The Stick

The Stick

A history, a celebration, an elegy

Bruce Dowbiggin

Macfarlane Walter & Ross
Toronto

Macfarlane Walter & Ross
An Affiliate of McClelland & Stewart Ltd.
37A Hazelton Avenue
Toronto, Canada M5R 2E3
www.mwandr.com

National Library of Canada cataloguing in publication data

Dowbiggin, Bruce
The stick : a history, a celebration, an elegy

Includes index.
ISBN 1-55199-055-5

1. Hockey – equipment and supplies.   I. Title.
GV848.4.C3D68 2001   796.962'028   C2001-901890-8

Picture credits: page 235 courtesy of Dai Skuse; page 242 Reuters/Bob Strong; all others courtesy of the Hockey Hall of Fame, Toronto.

Winter Sun The Dumfounding, Poems 1940-1966 by Margaret Avison and *Garden of Folly* by Stephen Leacock. Used by permission, McClelland & Stewart Ltd. *The Canadian Publishers.*

"Hockey Players" by Al Purdy from *Beyond Remembering: The Collected Poems of Al Purdy*. Copyright © 2000 by Al Purdy. Reproduced with the permission of Harbour Publishing.

Lines from *The Hockey Sweater and Other Stories* by Roch Carrier copyright © 1979 by House of Anansi Press. Reproduced with the permission of the publisher.

Macfarlane Walter & Ross gratefully acknowledges support for its publishing program from the Canada Council for the Arts, the Ontario Arts Council, and the Government of Canada through the Book Publishing Industry Development Program.

Printed and bound in Canada

To Ian, Peter, Gordie, and Stew
"Hey, who wants to take shots?"

CONTENTS

ACKNOWLEDGEMENTS

The Stick grew from a brief passage in my last book, *Of Ice and Men*. My editor, Gary Ross, suggested we expand on the idea of sticks as a quintessentially Canadian symbol. The next thing I knew I was wrapped up in electrical tape and fibreglass.

I have been guided in this project by a number of people both inside and outside hockey. Many of them are named in the book, but I would like to cite a few for their contributions. Gus Thorson, equipment manager of the Calgary Flames, was always available to point out a stick rep or a unique stick pattern. The company reps and researchers were always patient with requests and questions.

For the Mi'kmaq origins of the stick I owe a debt of thanks to James Raffan's fine work on canoes, *Bark, Skin and Cedar*, and the excellent research of Dr. Garth Vaughan, an all-star of research, in *The Puck Starts Here*. Brian Logie was an invaluable source for the history of Hespeler and the

Ontario factories. Dan Brunton helped warm up "God's Zamboni." Gilles Pelchat's history of Sher-Wood provided insights into that company's history and Carl Brewer helped open a window on the Finnish hockey stick industry. Stephen Murphy of Bauer/Nike guided the way to the new universe of composites and aluminum. Finally, Mike Gillis and Rich Winter gave good counsel on players and their predilections.

Cathy Jonasson of Bruce Mau Design is one of my three stars. She opened the door to the artists and creative people who made this journey unique. My researchers Richard Martyn and Stewart Dowbiggin were tireless in tracking down the companies and providing interviews.

Gary Ross and Jan Walter once again made writing a book seem like a tolerable experience when everyone knows it is one of the ordeals of hell. Thanks to Adrienne Guthrie for handling the details at the office, and to Wendy Thomas for her careful copyedit.

Finally, my family – Meredith, Evan, Rhys, and Clare – were my power play and my penalty killers throughout the making of *The Stick*. You win with special teams.

INTRODUCTION

A father and young son stand in the gloom beneath the seats at Maple Leaf Gardens. The boy wears the tricoleur of the Montreal Canadiens sweater. "Roy" is stencilled above the number 33 on his back. The boy's eyes are as big as the cavernous old arena itself. For the last three hours he's watched his heroes play the Maple Leafs, supplying non-stop play-by-play in his choirboy voice. Now, as the roar of the crowd escapes onto Carlton Street, he stands in the privileged position beside the Zamboni, waiting for his heroes to file past on their way to the cramped dressing rooms in Conn Smythe's old pile of bricks. He will be *this* close to his beloved Habs.

For the father, too, there's a sense of anticipation. He can recall an evening when he was seven years old, at the Forum in Montreal. He stood beside the ice with *his* father, waiting to see the great Gordie Howe, followed by Alex Delvecchio and Normie Ullman. The entire Red Wings team passed before him in their white jerseys with red trim, each player holding his Northland stick just so in the palm of a brown leather glove, like a bishop's staff.

He can still recall the words that passed that long-ago night between his father and Bill Gadsby, the Red Wings ageless defenceman. They might have come down from Olympus.

"Hey, Bill!" his father had shouted to the veteran rearguard, who'd just come over from the New York Rangers. "How you doing? How's everything?"

"Good. How's Edna?"

"Fine. Terry says hi."

"Say hello for me. Sorry, I've got to get the bus. . . . We'll see you soon."

"Go get 'em, Bill."

In all the mysteries that made up my father's life, I added this: friend to an NHL hockey player. They'd shared a duck blind one night in Saskatchewan, my father explained in an offhand way – as if he went hunting every day with an NHL star. Could I keep the news till recess the next day or would I simply burst?

Now it's a new generation of father and son at rinkside. What will this son remember of his first NHL game, if this father can't connect them to the theatre, the high mass of hockey? There's no one on the Canadiens with whom he can strike up a casual conversation. The players, passing by, seem even taller and more massive than he remembers from his own childhood. Stepping into their way would be like stepping in front of a semi on the 401. Whom to approach?

At the moment of the father's despair, Montreal tough guy

Chris Nilan comes rumbling down the rubber mat in that pigeon-toed, John Wayne gait players use to get around off the ice. Nilan – whose epic playoff fights with Dale Hunter of the Nordiques at the old Colisée were so bloodthirsty they made your hair stand on end – is bathed in sweat and gore from his battles with the Maple Leafs, and is the last player a father would expect to take note of a little boy in a carefully pressed Canadiens sweater standing in the wings of Maple Leaf Gardens.

But Nilan stops before the boy. A gentle smile lights up his warrior's face. "So – the Canadiens ya' favourite team?" he asks in his soft New England accent. The tiny voice that had filled the air all evening with questions and commentary and high-pitched squeals goes silent. Nilan recognizes the signs of panic, the awe his presence has created.

"Here," he says, "take this." He thrusts a white "Canadien" model stick into the little hands and tousles the boy's hair with a sweaty glove. Then, without a backward glance, he's gone down the hallway and into the visitors' dressing room.

The boy, now taller than his father, still has that Nilan stick; it leans against the wall amid the clutter of a teenager's bedroom. For reference, perhaps, or as a bragging point in the one-upsmanship of school, but also as a talisman, a reminder of a night with his father, and of the game that binds Canadians over the generations.

One evening, finding himself in his son's room, the father picks up the stick to feel its heft, its perfect balance, the cool smoothness of the shaft. Running his palm over the carefully taped knob, he wonders at the nicks and black marks produced by Nilan's combat – wonders, too, where his youth has gone, the hours on an outdoor rink, the crack of the stick, the recoil, the puck rocketing toward the boards and then the sweet sound of impact magnified by the snowy quiet – a noise that speaks to anyone who has skated late into the night of Canadian winter.

Gordie Howe, as Canadian as Precambrian red jasper, can still recall the excitement generated by his first stick. "Ab Welsh was my hero," Howe wrote in his autobiography. "He played for Saskatoon, on the senior team, and he took me in the dressing room one day. And he asked, 'Which way do you shoot, kid?' I said, 'Right, sir.' He said 'Good' and handed me a stick. Boy, that meant a heck of a lot to me. I came out of there fifteen feet tall. He didn't know it, but he made a friend for life that day. I guess that was about the first new stick I ever had. It was a beautiful stick." Whenever Howe held a wooden stick, he held something of Canada's legacy in his hands. Wooden sticks were as Canadian as maple syrup and the call of the loon.

Robert Fulford has written that Canadians are "slowly obliterating the country's symbolic landscape." The wooden stick seems destined to join those symbols, overtaken by progress, our affinity for the new. In the garage, the teenager has another stick, a sleek, wood-grain model from Branches, taped and game-ready. At first glance, the blond, handsome stick seems the epitome of natural engineering, wood's perfect union of strength and flexibility. Instead, it's a perfect fraud, a graphite copy from California, cold and efficient, with only a trace of wood in its curved blade. Shots leap off this pricey counterfeit like rockets, and growing numbers of

NHL stars nowadays will use only graphite. In fact, graphite is sweeping aside traditional sticks made of ash and elm just as surely as titanium heads and graphite shafts displaced persimmon heads and hickory shafts in golf clubs. Even diehards such as Al MacInnis, the veteran St. Louis defenceman who has the hardest shot in the NHL, have abandoned wood for the new materials.

Whether graphite or wood, the hockey stick will never entirely lose its symbolic place. In the mid-1990s, David Adams Richards, the Giller prize–winning novelist who grew up along the Miramichi River in New Brunswick, was working on a book in the fishing village of Denia on the Mediterranean coast of Spain. It was the time of the so-called Turbot War between Canada and Spain over fishing quotas on the Grand Banks. Bus drivers and waiters in a town that had depended for centuries on fish caught in the distant waters of Canada were reluctant to serve or even speak to him and his family.

"The Spanish didn't know what to do with us and we didn't know what to do, either," Richards recalls. "We stayed more and more to ourselves. My son, John, and I would play hockey with bamboo sticks on the patio all day. Kind of like road hockey, except we didn't have real sticks. John would wear his Montreal Canadiens sweater and sometimes we'd convince my wife, Peg, to play in the nets.

"There was a Spanish woman named Monty who had rented a villa nearby with her two children. She'd become friendly with us while she looked for a house. When the Turbot War came, it was awkward but she didn't want to lose that friendship. One day her girlfriend arrived from

Switzerland, and she'd brought a hockey stick with 'Team Canada' written on it. Monty's friend had found the stick in Switzerland, and Monty had asked her to bring it for us. It was a great thing she did. It symbolized so much – the friendship, the understanding of who we were as Canadians in another part of the world. It brought home what our culture really was."

CHAPTER 1

THE FOREST FLOOR

Roots have spread out from the Tree of the Great Peace, one to the north, one to the east, one to the south, and one to the west. The name of these roots is The Great White Roots and their nature is Peace and Strength.

The Great Law of the Five Nations

The legend of the hockey stick – like so much of Canadian history – begins with the First Nations. The Mi'kmaq elders tell of Gisoolg, the Great Spirit, creating the world. He was aided by Nisgam, the sun – giver of life, of light and heat. Ootsitgamoo was the earth, keeper of its abundant riches of water and land.

One day, Gisoolg used a thunderbolt to create Glooscap, the first man, from the sand. But Glooscap lay stuck on the beach – his feet pointing west toward the setting sun, his right hand pointing north – watching Nisgam cross the sky each day. Glooscap grew restless to walk among the birds and trees and waters and asked Nisgam to free him. With another crack of lightning Nisgam freed Glooscap to travel the earth in his stone canoe. After a time of wandering, he landed in the area believed to be the Annapolis Basin of Nova Scotia.

Glooscap went into the hardwood forest. From this abundance he gave the Mi'kmaq people the birch-bark canoe, the bow, the basket, and the other gifts of the forest. The Mi'kmaq became accomplished carvers and workers of wood. They travelled around what is now the Maritimes and Maine in search of food and materials from which to create their handicrafts. In winter they made skates from the jaw-bones of animals, which allowed them to move across the ice. And they played a game called Oochamkunutk, using carved alder sticks.

At first, the arrival of the white men did little to disturb this traditional life. The white people traded with the Mi'kmaq, but the newcomers largely clung to the shorelines and rivers. The forests still belonged to the First Nations. There were clashes of culture, but the Europeans kept to their spaces and the Mi'kmaq to theirs amidst the oak and elm and stately white pine, some reaching as high as 240 feet. And so it might have continued had it not been for the wars across the sea.

The popular view of Canadian history tells us that voyageurs in their sleek canoes, trading with the natives and surveying a continent, created what we now call Canada. Or that the hardy fishermen of the Grand Banks were the colonizers of Canada. But the wealth created by these industries wound up in Europe, an ocean away from their source. Without landed wealth, you can have no nation. That changed one winter's day early in the nineteenth century. In the vast forest, a woodsman first swung his axe at virgin white pine to fell a mast for a ship of the line in the Royal Navy. By the time he was finished clearing the forest, Canada was a nation.

As the nineteenth century dawned, Canada, despite hundreds of years of European settlement, was still a new coat, barely lived in. India, not Canada, was the jewel in King George's crown. Compared to the awakening bull to the south, the United States of America, Canada lay like a sleeping dog at the hearth of civilization, happy in its isolation.

In France, an ambitious Napoleon had commenced a nineteenth-century version of an arms race, building war ships to challenge Pax Britannica. Mindful of its hegemony on the waves, Britain was forced to keep pace with the supply of ships in France. A seventy-four–gun ship of the line in the Royal Navy required 2,600 tons of timber in the hull alone – the equivalent of 700 large trees – to say nothing of the three 120-foot masts and the fittings.

The Crown was finding it nearly impossible to find enough wood. Having stripped and burned its own forests long ago, Imperial Britain depended on the Baltic countries and the vast New England forests of America. The Revolutionary War of 1776 – partly incited by England's management of the American forests – had put the towering ninety-foot American pines needed for masts out of reach. When Napoleon blockaded the Baltic in November of 1806, the British needed a cheap, expedient solution.

The forests of Prussia and Scandinavia were off-limits to Britain; the nearly endless stands of white pine, elm, spruce, and maple in Canada were not. The supply seemed endless, transportation costs were low (icy roads through snow-bound forests were the perfect highway to deliver the huge cut logs to market). And Canada's river network was ideal to float the logs to ports in Quebec and Halifax. So Britain's trading ships were turned away from the Baltic and directed to the northern shores of North America.

"I remember in May of 1809," recalled an awed John Sewell, a Quebec merchant, "the appearance round the point at Levis of the first fleet of British ships coming in search of our oak, pine, spars and masts for England's navies – royal and merchant." That fleet was followed by many more, seeking to fill their hulls with as much squared timber as they could drag from the forests.

By 1810, lumber had surpassed fur trading as the dominant industry in the fledgling colonies. In 1811, the Atlantic Provinces shipped 4,000 masts of pine, while 500 ships set sail from Quebec City with 75,000 loads of white pine and white oak and 23,000 masts. By 1820, the Canadian forests were supplying eighty per cent of Britain's timber. The St. Lawrence, Ottawa, Miramichi, Madawaska, St. John, Saguenay, Petawawa, and St. Maurice rivers roiled with enormous timber rafts headed for use in Britain. Where rapids and waterfalls got in the way, the timber kings built slipways and canals.

Britain's need for squared timber supplied Canada with its first settled economy, and the prosperity fuelled the emerging nation. Lumbermen such as Philemon Wright, in

Bytown, and William Davidson, an expatriate Scot, on the Miramichi, guaranteed that their homeland would rule the waves and that they would rule Canadian commerce. "What is the world made of?" asked one of Wright's friends. "White pine!" The names of the great lumber tycoons from that era – Price, Booth, Eddy – are ingrained in Canadian history.

The promise of fortunes to be made in the forests of Canada drew men from Britain and its colonies in the first half of the nineteenth century. They brought their dreams and hopes and families. John Egan, an Irish emigrant, commanded an army of 3,800 men and 400 teams of horses to get his wood down the Ottawa River. In the mid-1840s, he was sending fifty-five rafts of timber to market each summer.

The Irish soldiers and settlers who had arrived in Nova Scotia at the dawn of the eighteenth century also brought with them the game of hurley. Played on an open field with a crooked wooden stick and a ball, it was not unlike the Mi'kmaq's game of Oochamkunutk. In the winter climate of their new home, the Europeans adapted their games and equipment for use on ice. Soon the two cultures were playing Alchamadijk, as the Mi'kmaq called it. The white men would call the new game hockey. And the best sticks for this new game came from the carvers of the Mi'kmaq.

Even in the harsh fluorescent light of the basement vault in the Hockey Hall of Fame in downtown Toronto, Fred "Cyclone" Taylor's teak-brown stick – with its flowing inscriptions on the shaft and its fraying blade – still feels like magic. Taylor was hockey's first high-priced star, a piano tuner who, according to the local *Renfrew Journal,* "provided endless entertainment to the gallery" in the first two decades of the twentieth century. The 5-foot-8 speedster used this one-piece elm stick for almost two seasons – including the Stanley Cup–winning campaign of 1908 with Ottawa's fabled "Silver Seven." His gnarled, hand-carved stick is remarkably short and light, but, lying in the racks along with Gretzky, Howe, and Orr models, it has lost none of its ability to amaze a hockey fan. What's most remarkable about the stick – which has "Ottawa" carved into the blade to commemorate the 1908 Cup win – is its bowed shaft. It's as if Taylor had been trying to snap the stick in anger, but then decided to leave it in the shape he'd created, curved like a scythe. How much of this curve was Taylor's doing and how much is warpage is hard to determine, but it's the most striking exhibit in the stick vault.

Taylor received his nickname "Cyclone" from none other than Governor General Earl Grey (of CFL trophy fame), who remarked upon seeing the rover score four goals in one game, "He's a cyclone if ever I saw one." Taylor was also Canada's first "overpaid" athlete. The Renfrew Millionaires lured him away from Ottawa in 1909 for the princely sum of $5,200 – more than the salary of Prime Minister Wilfrid Laurier – and bitter Ottawa Senators fans labelled him "spoiled" as they hurled bottles, fruit, and horse apples at him when he made his return to the nation's capital in a Renfrew uniform. In revenge, Taylor executed the unprece-dented feat of scoring a goal against the Sens while skating backwards in a 17–2 Millionaires' spanking of Ottawa. Later in his career, Taylor went west to join more Millionaires, this time in Vancouver, where he rewrote the scoring records in the Pacific Coast Hockey Association, leading Vancouver to the Cup in 1915. The Cyclone whirled for ninety-four years – he turned the sod for the original Hall of Fame in Toronto in 1960 – after being named an MBE by King George for his work in World War II.

Taylor had learned his hockey in Listowel, Ontario, north of Stratford, and it's doubtful he ever met a Mi'kmaq carver from Nova Scotia. But he certainly knew their work. Any self-respecting hockey man of his day used one of their creations.

The first commercial sticks made by Mi'kmaq carvers were of hornbeam (also called ironwood in testament to its strength and durability). When the supply of hornbeam ran out, yellow birch became the tree of choice. Ideal trees had exposed roots that naturally grew out from the trunk in the angle of a stick blade – the Mi'kmaq called these "hockey roots." Roots contained the tree's hardest wood and, because the grain flowed naturally from trunk to root, they were perfect for the blade and the battering it was subject to. Second-growth wood – trees that had replaced the original stands – was considered best for sticks, because it combined the strength of first growth with the flexibility of a younger tree.

Raymond Cope and Sandy Julien, Mi'kmaq carvers on the Millbrook Reserve, near Truro, Nova Scotia, still remember their fathers setting off with horses and wagons to harvest "hockey wood" in the traditional way each fall, before the snow fell. The carvers would uproot a suitable tree, complete with root ball, for transport back to camp. A typical root slab might yield as many as three sticks; with several roots per tree, a fine specimen might yield a dozen sticks and good money for the Mi'kmaqs. The carvers outlined a stick on the wood, then used a two-handed square saw to cut out the depicted sticks. According to Garth Vaughan's history of the sport in Nova Scotia, *The Puck Starts Here*, the Mi'kmaq later adapted the metal springs of discarded gramophones to fashion blades for these saws. Rough-hewn sticks were dried over a stove. The carvers finished the job in the kitchen, using drawknives and crooked-knives to refine the blade and smooth the handle. After being sanded and oiled, the stick was ready for use or for shipment to hardware stores such as Phinney's or Creighton's in Halifax. Because they did not warp or bend (as steam-bent models did), one-piece sticks crafted in the Mi'kmaq way were unsurpassed until the 1920s, when two- and three-piece sticks were first produced by factories in Halifax and Ontario.

Vaughan, a retired doctor, lives in Windsor, Nova Scotia. He grew up hearing about Mi'kmaq sticks and the legendary carvers, and he went to the reserves near Truro to research his book. "I found a couple of people who knew all about it. They showed me pictures of their father as a carver, and they've still got his tools. They're going to give me one of the square saws for the museum we have in Windsor. Those saws are really something, like the prototype of a bandsaw or jigsaw. It looks like a picture frame that they just strung a little saw down the middle of. It was very exciting to discover them."

While some Mi'kmaq carved their sticks on the reserve, others gravitated to factories, such as the Pirate Hockey

Stick Company in Wolfville, Nova Scotia. The renowned carver Frank Toney, chief of the King's County Reserve, and his sons, Pat and Tom, were among the local woodsmen in the 1910s and 1920s who hand-carved sticks for the teams from Acadia University and surrounding towns. After the Pirate Sticks factory burned down later in the decade – the fate of many stick factories – Toney sold his sticks and carved baskets door to door or at local markets.

Hockey fan Tommy Sweet of Halifax recalls the Mi'kmaq selling their sticks along with other produce at the Saturday market for 25 or 50 cents as late as the 1920s. Sweet told Vaughan, "No two sticks were alike. You just picked out the one that best suited you." If you stayed long enough, and if the Mi'kmaq did not sell out their inventory, you could get a bargain at the end of the day.

Mi'kmaq sticks (then called Mic-Mac) travelled far and wide as the sport's popularity grew in the second half of the nineteenth century. The only identification at that time was on the blade, not the shaft; still, in hundreds of posed photos of the day, native-carved sticks are clearly identifiable. In one shot, the sons of Lord Stanley, donor of the famous cup, lounge insouciantly with their colleagues of the Rideau Hall Rebels of 1888, Mic-Mac sticks in hand. In another photo, this one showing the 1905 Toronto Marlboros, the players' precious Mic-Mac sticks are reverentially crossed at their feet.

Though the last commercial Mi'kmaq sticks were carved almost seventy-five years ago, some remain in circulation. Thanks to Vaughan's work, the Hockey Heritage Centre in Windsor, Nova Scotia, has a well-preserved 1920s specimen from Toney that was rescued from a barn in nearby Falmouth. And the Hockey Hall of Fame in Toronto has, besides Taylor's stick, models used by many of the game's original stars as early as the turn of the century.

If imitation is flattery, the Mi'kmaq stick received a great compliment from the Starr Manufacturing Company of Dartmouth, Nova Scotia. A manufacturer of nails, screws, nuts, and bolts long before Confederation, Starr later branched out into making skates to supply the sport of hockey that was fast emerging on the ponds and rivers of the province. The Starr skate brand became famous in 1865 when Starr's foreman, John Forbes, and his assistant, Thomas Bateman, invented the "spring skate," which allowed people to clamp skates on their boots. Soon screw-on blades were added – using Starr's own screws, naturally.

Like all companies that depended on mail-order business, Starr produced a catalogue of its products. To expand its hockey business, it got serious about the stick trade at the turn of the century, using the same plentiful stands of yellow birch near its Dartmouth headquarters that the Mi'kmaq used. Looking for a new name synonymous with hockey, Starr named the sticks Mic-Mac; they were made "to meet the requirements of the best players." While lacking the individuality of the originals, Starr's Mic-Macs were highly rated for their durability and their shape retention even when the weather turned mild and wet.

"The Mic-Mac hockey stick," reads an ad in the Eaton's catalogue from 1905. "Made of selected second-growth

Yellow Birch for forwards, defense and goal, the natural grain of the wood running with the curve of the blade. It possesses many advantages over the Steam-bent Stick. Some of its excellent features are: 1st – Stiffness and Lightness; 2nd – Will not fray at the bottom of the blade; 3rd – Keeps its correct shape; 4th – Correct in pattern and weight; 5th – Every stick carefully inspected before leaving the factory." At the bottom of the ad lies a warning. "The attention of Manufacturers and Dealers is drawn to the fact that our hockey sticks are fully covered in Ottawa, viz: the words Mic-Mac and Rex (another Starr stick line) as trade marks and the design of Rex as an industrial design. Infringers will be prosecuted."

Ads for Rex sticks – "the Expert's Favourites" – promised serrations on the handle to prevent slippage, and double-grooved blades "to insure accurate shooting and strengthen the stick." For added durability, the sticks were soaked in oil, giving them a dark, rich finish. The oil also made them virtually indestructible, even in the harsh, brutal conditions of what was an outdoor game. These Mic-Mac and Rex sticks might last a player two or three seasons, and specimens that look ready for use still turn up in basements or attics.

Not that they'd belong in today's game. A contemporary NHL player – 6-foot-9 Zdeno Chara of the Islanders, say, or 6-foot-5 Derian Hatcher of Dallas – would find one of these original Mic-Mac or Rex sticks comically short. The Rex was about forty-five inches long compared to the current NHL average of fifty-five inches, or the sixty-three inches that Chara uses. Modern players would also discover that Mic-Macs were downright inflexible. Slapping the puck would have all the feel of using an axe handle (staples of the same manufacturers). The hardwood surface, too, would be slippery in cold weather, making serrations or tape necessary to keep a firm grip on the stick. Some sticks featured a bowed shaft and a flat lie (the angle at which the blade meets the heel). Long before anyone thought to curve the blade, the Starr catalogue of 1906 has illustrations of Mic-Mac and Rex models with a pronounced curve in the shaft.

Imagine a rambunctious young Saskatchewan farm boy thumbing through the Eaton's catalogue of the day. While scheming for ways to make the 39 cents needed for a brand-new Mic-Mac, he might have tried carving his own in the meantime, based on the pictures in the catalogue. The Hockey Hall of Fame has a vintage photo showing George Loewen, a Saskatchewan farmer, and his family and friends on their skates for their annual New Year's Day hockey game on the local slough. The photographer has captured four men in caps and two women in ankle-length skirts carrying crude sticks fashioned from the alders that grew on the farm. The sticks are bent and gnarled, the blades of varying length and straightness, but they are unmistakably hockey sticks and – judging from the smiles – more than adequate for the task.

One-piece sticks of alder or yellow birch ruled the game for eight decades. Only a dwindling supply of hardwood trees in the years before World War II would bring about their demise.

For this Saskatchewan farm family in 1910, new hockey sticks
were as close as the nearest tree—they fashioned their own
models out of suitable roots.

CHAPTER 2

GOD'S ZAMBONI

A culture is no better than its woods.

W.H. Auden, "The Shield of Achilles," 1955

Stand on the banks of the Speed River in Hespeler, Ontario, not far from modern-day Kitchener. Imagine a wall of ice the height of a skyscraper creeping across what were once lush, subtropical lakes and forests teeming with life. The earth's climate has changed; the warmth that spawned those abundant life forms has vanished. Frigid temperatures have slowly built up this mountain of ice till it now encroaches year-round even at this southerly point. For 75,000 years, this unstoppable plough scrapes these rolling lands of everything – trees, boulders, arable land – pushing it south into what is now the United States.

God's Zamboni ploughs enormous furrows, flattens mountains, and deposits entire formations at its farthest advance to the south. Long Island and Cape Cod are created by its inexorable progress. This era – which finally ends 10,000 years ago with the ice cap retreating to the North Pole – is known by geologists as the Wisconsin Ice Age, after the point in modern-day Wisconsin at which the ice wall finally abated. At the peak of the Wisconsonian era, three-fifths of all the world's ice lies on North America.

A spiking of the earth's temperatures, begun 40,000 years earlier, has warmed the earth enough to finally stop God's Zamboni in its tracks. Slowly the ice recedes northward. The enormous weight of the retreating pack and its melting water carves out many of the hills and riverbeds surrounding what will one day become Hespeler in Waterloo County. As God's Zamboni creeps back to the polar ice cap, the melt-water floods the Great Lakes basin and an enormous lake is formed in the centre of the continent. Beneath this watery surface, the earth's tectonic plates are in constant motion, shunting and shoving, throwing up new mountain ranges in the west, wearing down the mountains of the east.

By 14,000 B.C., water has collected in the Great Lakes and in the multitude of rivers and streams that feed the greatest reservoir of fresh inland water on the globe. But the land, which once boasted dinosaurs and warm tropical forests that stretched skyward, has been scraped bald. At first, the thin soil can support only ferns, mosses, lichens, and other simple plant forms. Later, shrubby softwoods such as dogwood and alder take root in the compost left behind by the early life forms. The wind carries yet more seeds and spores from far-off forests, while deer and migrating birds come to feed on the berries, leaving behind the seeds that will grow into the great hardwoods beside Lake Erie and Lake Ontario.

In this evolving terrain, woods will eventually stretch from the Great Lakes down the Appalachian Mountains to the present state of Georgia, what we now know as the Carolinian zone. It's said that a squirrel could travel its lifetime through the branches of white pines on this highway of trees without ever touching another species of tree or setting foot on the ground.

By the time of recorded human history (the fifth century B.C.), the forest floor on the northern limit of the Carolinian zone is also home to white ash, maple, rock elm, trembling aspen, beech, oak, and a host of other species, each struggling for a piece of the tree canopy above which is found sun and heat and life. The forest is periodically cleansed by fire and ice and snow, but emerges stronger each time from nature's pruning. Gradually, humans with Mongoloid features move into the area north of the Great Lakes. How they made the long trek from Asia is hotly debated, but when they see the trees and lakes and rivers, they know they are home. For hundreds, perhaps thousands, of years – until the Europeans arrive – they will be masters of the area.

While the natives worship and draw sustenance from their natural surroundings, the European settlers who arrive around 1800 cut down whatever trees get in their way. Men such as Abram Clemens – a United Empire Loyalist from Pennsylvania who arrived in what would be Hespeler in 1809 – convert the stands of ash, oak, elm, and pine to houses, furniture, wagons, and timber for export. When the fecund forest proves too abundant, they simply burn the excess to make room for farmland. The endless forest begins to disappear into furrowed fields and bustling villages.

This emerging lumber trade also produces a cultural shift. Young men hungry for profit and adventure leave the drudgery of the plough or the shop back in Europe to try their luck in British North America. Often, they bring wives and families with them to the New World. Catherine Parr Traill, who – with her sister Susanna Moodie – chronicled life in early Ontario from 1833 to 1899, remembered the stark scene that greeted a new English bride in a fledgling town near present-day Peterborough. "She . . . turned with deep disgust from the unsightly prospect of half-cleared fields, disfigured by charred stumps and surrounded by scorched and blackened trees, in the midst of which lay her new home. Where was the charming rural village her husband had spoken of with pride and delight? Here was only a sawmill – never a pleasant sight – heaps of newly sawn boards, and all the debris of bark and chips, and the skeleton frames of unfinished buildings scattered without order over the rough ground."

Farther west, on the site of what was to become New Hamburg, Ontario, Amish Mennonites under Josiah Gushman built a sawmill and gristmill alongside Smith's Creek (now the Nith River) in 1834 to exploit the forests. For a time, the young community of Cassel thrived, until Gushman made a visit to nearby Galt to watch a travelling circus. He brought home cholera, and most of the village population perished along with him.

Others quickly took their places in Cassel and in thousands of other communities. Their names spoke of the settlers' origins – Dresden, Berlin, London, Paris, Exeter, Culloden,

New Dundee, New Hamburg. As long as there was a river to power the sawmill and an endless supply of pine, ash, and rock elm for timber, the towns prospered. The area's commercial opportunities were enhanced when this area – from modern-day Kitchener down through London to the shores of the St. Clair River – was linked by the Grand Trunk Railway, which took wood products to markets in Toronto and Montreal and the United States.

In many small Ontario towns – Ayr, Ingersoll, Wallaceburg, St. Mary's, Waterloo – hockey-stick making began as an afterthought, a sideline for manufacturers of wood products looking to boost sales, maximize production, and keep their employees working year-round. Some firms – E.B. Salyerd in Preston, for one – were making sticks as early as 1887. Others followed a more circuitous path to stick making. The factory housing the Monarch Stick Company, for instance, had its origins in New Hamburg as a wagon manufacturer in 1902. It became a furniture factory in 1907, suffered insolvency, became a second furniture operation in 1923, endured more insolvency, then evolved into a manufacturer of truck bodies and other wood products. Finally, in April 1934, Clayton Berger moved the hockey-stick operation he'd run in his father's nearby factory to the property on Arnold Street in New Hamburg. There he produced Monarch hockey sticks until a catastrophic fire in 1954 reduced the plant to ashes and ended the story of Monarch Sticks.

One business, however, symbolizes the scope and impact of Ontario-made sticks. Since 1905, the stick factory on the banks of the Speed River has had no peer for longevity or for the renown of its sticks. Ever since the Cyclone Taylor era, the unhurried town of Hespeler (amalgamated as part of Cambridge, Ontario, in 1972) has been the heart of the stick industry. In its early days it was one of many such companies making sticks, along with brooms, axles, and farm implements; eventually, many of its competitors moved their facilities into the brick building by the Speed. Today, Bauer/Nike is the resident manufacturer on site, turning out wood-laminate sticks for a global market in a modern building across the street from the original factory. But the presence of a multinational giant like Nike is just a footnote in the history and significance of a place once swept by God's Zamboni.

Trees in Canada describes the rock elm (or cork elm) as "the hardest, heaviest, strongest and toughest of the elms; wood formerly used where such features are essential, e.g. for making piano frames and hockey sticks, but no longer available in commercial quantities." British ship builders loved rock elm, because its interlaced fibres made it virtually impossible to split. As well, it was buoyant and watertight. After so many years of supplying the furniture and timber industries, rock elm is now a rare tree in Ontario.

But it grew in abundance when Jacob Hespeler arrived in what was known as New Hope, Ontario, in 1845. A businessman, he'd invented a faster process for making vinegar back in Preston, Ontario. When he found he couldn't make money as fast as he made vinegar, he moved his attentions to New Hope and began buying land around the village.

By 1858, the year the town's name was changed to Hespeler to reflect his civic contributions, Jacob Hespeler ran a spinning mill, a cooper's workshop, and the inevitable sawmill. While settlers had built the first sawmill in the area as early as 1830, it was Hespeler's mill and other business holdings that gave the small town its foothold on history. Soon, the furniture and lumber operations would vie with the Dominion Woolens and Worsteds Company – later Dominion Textile – as the prime sources of employment in the area. (Dominion Woolens became the largest firm of its type in Canada.) The long stone buildings that housed the knitting companies with their hundreds of employees still sit on the south bank of the Speed, ghostly reminders of a glorious era.

On the north side of the river, next to the dilapidated railway station, stands the imposing original red-brick factory of the Hespeler Wood Specialty Company, which now houses a furniture factory. The smell of sawdust and green wood still hangs in the air, even though the hockey-stick operation moved across Sheffield Street to low-slung, modern facilities in the 1970s.

Hespeler Wood Specialty Products was formed in this building by Z.A. Hall in 1905 to make coaster-wagon sleighs, implement handles, and hockey sticks for an emerging nation of farmers and sportsmen. Its products reflected Edwardian confidence in the future, spurred by the moral superiority of an Imperial realm that never saw the setting of the sun. Hespeler Wood Specialty Products was designed to build the Dominion and bring glory to the Empire.

The first hockey sticks made in Hespeler were one-piece models, from bolts of rock elm six or seven feet long and six inches thick. Most of the wood was sourced locally, but as demand increased, the wood came from farther afield in Canada and the United States. The quality of the wood was assessed by the foreman as it arrived on the train spur, with the best samples – those with clear, straight grains – going to professional or expensive models of stick. Wood with knots or irregularities was directed to low-end sticks or to axe handles.

The bolts that arrived at Hespeler were bent using steam, then held in place by massive clamps that shaped the softened wood under great tension. (The manufacturers used the same spring-loaded clamps to bend wood for furniture and piano frames.) Employees used a large hammer to release the metal rods holding the wood, standing clear as the contraption released its pent-up energy.

After being dried in a kiln to a moisture content of no more than eight per cent, the re-shaped bolts were cut into as many as six sticks each. Finished sticks had their blades dipped in varnish to help prevent cracking. When the stick was ready for market, a paper label was affixed to the top of the shaft with details of who made it and where. Due to the vagaries of such haphazard labelling, few of the sticks that survive today have any identification.

Like all steamed sticks, the Hespeler models gradually reverted to their original shape, a constant problem in warm weather or on soft ice (less a problem in the first decades of the century, when the Stanley Cup was usually awarded by the middle of March). Young players used electrical tape to keep the sticks from warping. They also brought them into the house between games to dry out. At prices that ranged from 45 cents a dozen up to $4.05 for a goalie stick – not inconsequential sums for the day – it paid to make a stick last as long as possible.

By 1922, when it employed twenty-five workers, Hespeler Wood Specialty had become an innovator in the stick industry, patenting a three-piece goalie stick (first popularized by St. Mary's). Until then, goalie sticks had simply been defencemen's sticks with extra wood tacked atop the blade or shaft. The Hespeler innovation placed extra wood on both sides of the shaft, giving the stick the paddle shape it has today. With supplies of rock elm dwindling in Ontario – elm is slower to regenerate than other commercial woods – the Hespeler people got to thinking about how to create a multipiece regular stick as well. In the 1920s, the manufacturing process wasted as much harvested wood as it used; if a process could be found to insert the blade into a slot on the heel of the stick, more plentiful woods, such as white ash, could also be incorporated. The shortage of elm was becoming acute, and only so much of the rising costs for wood could be passed on to buyers. Innovation didn't take long.

In 1922, St. Mary's was the first to produce two-part sticks, which they marketed under the trade names Supreme and Canada. By 1925, Hespeler had two patents of its own on a two-piece stick. The blade was inserted into a mortise joint on the heel of the shaft, then glued. Hespeler also obtained a patent for a heel joint that was the forerunner of the three-part stick.

The first models encountered setbacks; glues used to hold the blades either failed or cracked in cold weather. Shipments by train to western Canada sometimes turned into high-priced kindling when the glues dried out or froze en route.

Gradually, the two-piece stick became standard, relegating custom-carved models to attics and barns. (Monarch used a metal rivet to hold the joint together. This model was known – for obvious reasons – as the shin buster.) Not only did the two-piece stick make better use of available wood, it was lighter and had greater flex in the shaft. As players grew stronger, this allowed them to shoot harder and with greater accuracy. These innovations came with a price: the first spliced sticks cost $8 a dozen in 1928, rising to $10 a dozen by 1930.

In the booming economic times of the 1920s, there was room for competition in the young Ontario market. By 1930, the stick industry boasted Salyerds in Preston, Hilborn in Ayr, St. Mary's Wood Specialty Products in St. Mary's, and Monarch in New Hamburg. Each had its niche. Hilborn, whose name was known across the country thanks to distribution by CCM and Eaton's, was the first to supply custom sticks to NHLers, such as the rambunctious Cleghorn brothers, Odie and Sprague. St. Mary's was known as the hockey wing of the famous baseball-bat makers. In 1887 Salyerds had brought out the Salyerd Special, the first manufactured Ontario stick, and the company had success with the Boy's Red – perhaps the first painted stick. Monarch shipped sticks under the Maroon and Canadian labels to the Montreal NHL franchises of the same names and supplied special three-piece sticks for George Hainsworth, the great Canadiens goalie.

But the stock market crash of 1929 and the subsequent international economic collapse dried up demand for goods and eliminated jobs in all industries. Hockey was not exempted. Before the Depression was over, the Maroons,

Brooklyn Americans, Pittsburgh Pirates, Philadelphia Quakers, and the venerable Ottawa Senators would all disappear, leaving only six NHL franchises for the next quarter century.

A similar contraction hit the wood-products business in Ontario. In 1930, the holding company for Seagram's (which became fabulously rich during Prohibition in the United States) was flush with cash and looking to diversify. It already owned Waterloo Wood Products, and Canada Barrels and Kegs; in 1930 it purchased Hespeler Wood Specialties. In 1931, it bought the Hilborn Company; in 1933, the St. Mary's Company was added; in 1934, Salyerds joined the fold. In each case, employees and equipment were transferred to the red-brick factory in Hespeler, and the hybrid hockey-stick maker was rechristened Hespeler St. Mary's Wood Specialty Products – to take advantage of both the hockey-stick legacy of Hespeler and the fame of St. Mary's baseball bats.

Besides sticks and bats, the new company also tried its hand at making skis. In 1930, Adolph Anderson, a Norwegian immigrant, was brought to Hespeler from White River, Ontario, north of Lake Superior, to oversee the making of cross-country skis and other products. Adolph brought along his family of eight, including fifteen-year-old Walter. "When we lived there, we weren't near the river," recalls Walter Anderson, now closing in on ninety, sitting in his Wallaceburg, Ontario, kitchen. "We were up on the hill – Jacobs Street, if I'm not mistaken, by the United Church."

Young Walter was soon working on the production line near his father and two of his brothers for 15 cents an hour – not a bad wage in the Depression, when work of any kind was appreciated. "We'd work about fifty hours a week," he says, rubbing fingers gnarled by arthritis and forty-five years in the stick business. "A nine-hour day and then Saturday morning for 15 cents an hour. That's what I started with."

The men on the line at Hespeler next to Anderson were expected to work any number of machines – band saw, rip saw, joiner, drum sander, steaming tank – but young Walter's first work was less demanding. "I used to put the labels on sticks. It was just flour and water and mix it all up into a glue and spread it on the paper and just wrap it on – put it around the stick as a label. Then stamping them and tying them up – I got piecework on that. Sometimes I made $10 in a week. I'd say Spalding was our biggest customer. They shipped all over. And I remember we shipped down to Montreal quite a bit. Kresge's was one place I sent to, a lot of the boys' sticks and so on. Come on, I'll show you something."

Anderson leads his visitor to the basement of his tidy home on the bank of the Thames River. On one wall hangs a framed advertisement for Louisville sticks. It reads: "One of the best stick handlers in the business has never played pro hockey. His name is Walter Anderson." It's a memento from later in his career, when he was the stick maker for Gordie Howe, Mickey Redmond, and many other Louisville clients. Anderson pulls down a Redmond model from its perch next to the advertisement. "See the grain here?" he asks. "Straight grain. That's what you're looking for. Now that's a straight grain and stiff enough. That's what we used. Ash. If it isn't straight-grained, if you have a knot in it or something, you leaned on the thing and it would break. I learned about grading wood from my dad. You had to scale the lumber when they used to bend it." Anderson became adept at grading timber by eye. His astute judgements bailed out a rookie factory owner years later.

"I remember the first load the guy sent me from Quebec," recalls Jack Lacey, who employed Anderson at Wally and Louisville sticks in the 1950s and '60s. "Walter took one look at it – he checked every load that came in – and said, 'This guy figures you're new and he's trying to take you. This is just garbage.' So I called the guy and gave him hell and we sent the load back."

The Andersons didn't remain long in Hespeler. The company got out of the ski business, then merged with the other firms. "A couple of their foremen came down with them, too," recalls Walter. "My dad didn't get along with them, so he moved out and went to New Hamburg. Dad got established up there so I went, too. Once we got into New Hamburg, we got burned out. Then we went on to Ingersoll. We moved into a casket factory and they had all the machines – the band saws, the planers, even a kiln. So we were right at home there." Eventually, in the 1960s, Walter Anderson made his way west to Wallaceburg and worked at the Wally sticks operation until his retirement in 1980.

Another young fellow who worked in the local stick factories went on to become a celebrity, on the ice and then off it. "There were three or four hockey-stick plants near Kitchener, where I'm from," recalls Howie Meeker, now retired in Parksville, British Columbia. "We had the Hespeler plant and one in New Hamburg. We used to go up there and work – carry wood out of the kiln, things like that. They'd give us cracked hockey sticks they couldn't sell."

Sticks would soon become much easier to obtain for the young man who became the NHL's Rookie of the Year in 1947. "My dad had a job – it was at Kuntz's Brewery. They made all kinds of pop and soft drinks. He had a truck and made deliveries to all the small towns around us – Elmira, Galt, Preston, Hespeler. One year, one of the companies came out with a promotion – so many bottle caps and they'd give you a free stick. All of a sudden, my dad's warehouse was full of hockey sticks. So my friends, everybody I played with, we had all kinds of sticks."

Though demand was battered by the Depression, Hespeler Wood Products continued producing sleek, laminated two-piece sticks. One model bore a familiar name, the Mic-Mac, which became available when Starr Manufacturing got out of the stick business in the 1930s.

The Mic-Mac became the stick of choice for a muscular young man who grew up on a farm near Belleville, Ontario, in the 1940s and 1950s. "Hespeler made the best sticks," recalls Bobby Hull, whose 610 career NHL goals puts him tenth on the all-time list – just behind son Brett. "Blue Flash, Green Flash, Hespeler Mic-Mac – they're the best sticks I used back then. I used one all season. My dad would buy it for me, because all my money went into the bank my brother-in-law welded for me so I couldn't get at it. Later, I lived near Hespeler, and played Junior B in Woodstock and Galt when I was fourteen or fifteen."

Backed by Seagram's, Hespeler Wood Products survived the Depression and World War II. Wood was scarce, buyers were scarce, and workers were headed off to the Army. By 1947, however, peacetime had revived a business that often seemed ready to collapse. "Today, this concern is turning out wood items to the tune of 1,000,000 units a year," boasted the program for an Old Boys Reunion that year. "Axes, picks, sledgehammers, hockey sticks, and baseball bats are the mainstays of the plant, shipped around the world."

Post-war prosperity also brought a major change in the wood used in the stick. Rock elm, used in automobile spokes and hubs as well as sticks, was on the wane; the ideal limestone-based terrain for this slow-growing species was being converted to pasture and residential use. Its wonderful qualities as a weight-bearing wood proved its undoing.

Manufacturers turned to white ash. More plentiful than elm, it grew in great stands in eastern Canada and the northeastern United States. White ash was also revered by native Canadians; the Algonkin legend talks of the World Ash, from which the first man emerged.

Wood is made of two principal substances: cellulose, which makes wood flexible, and lignin, a polyphenol that makes it hard. A tree with minimal lignin will be flexible but soft. For this reason the paper industry likes balsam or spruce, trees with long fibres but smaller amounts of lignin, which must be extracted. Cotton, linen, rayon, and cellophane are nearly all pure cellulose. On the other hand, hard woods such as hickory or black locust have short fibres and considerable lignin. The tightly knitted fibres are so strong and hard to compress that the English Navy used them for bolting the planks of wooden ships.

White ash has the ideal mix of cellulose for flexibility and lignin for durability. It's strong, but not as heavy as hickory or oak; it's pliant, but not as whippy as alder or poplar; and it's light, though not as weak as maple or linden. No wonder the famed naturalist Donald Culross Peattie wrote in the 1940s, "So far as concerns the trees of northeastern North America, the White Ash is nature's last word."

White ash was also easy to regenerate. Where a stand of oak would take 150 years from planting to harvesting, marketable white ash could be harvested in 25 years from second-growth trees. White ash in a virgin tract can soar 175 feet and live 300 years with a trunk 5 feet or more in diameter, yet commercial white ash can be harvested at a much smaller size. The pale sapwood that retail buyers prefer comes from second-growth trees as small as a foot in diameter, when the ratio of sapwood to heartwood is greatest. Today, most white ash is taken from tree farms, not virgin forests, for delivery to a small number of firms that specialize in ash products. For this reason, you're not likely to see much ash in your local woodlot.

If the Original Six NHL era, from 1942 to 1967, represented the golden age of hockey, those same years – when white ash was king – were also golden for the stick makers. Factories could specialize in hockey sticks and make a profit. As a result, implement handles and automobile parts were soon dropped in favour of hockey sticks at the Hespeler plant. One manufacturer happily recalls the joy of finding a factory that made bowling pins in a remote section of New Brunswick. After a little persuasion, it too was turning out hockey stick components instead of seven-ten splits.

The Hespeler plant was typical: there was a sawmill on the property, a kiln for drying the wood, and sheds or pallets for storing the raw product. Wood arrived in twenty-foot planks

In their heyday, the stick factories of southwestern Ontario—in
towns such as Hespeler, St. Mary's, and Wallaceburg—were the
center of the industry

three or four feet in diameter. The company's rip saws, band
saws, joiners, planers, drum sanders, and varnishers would
render these billets into hockey sticks. After minimal orna-
mentation – a red or green stripe was usually the extent of

it – the sticks were bundled and shipped to hardware and department store chains across the nation.

This traditional method of building a stick from white ash and glue would undergo only one significant change in almost half a century. In the 1950s, technicians at the Hespeler plant perfected the three-part stick, creating a separate heel joint about eight inches long that was glued to the base of the shaft. The blade was inserted into a groove in this heel joint, creating a stronger bond. The three-part stick ultimately paved the way for an offensive explosion in the NHL.

Before endorsements by NHL stars came to drive the retail market, CCM (in St. Jean d'Iberville, Quebec) and Northland (in Chaska, Minnesota) dominated the pro market. "We didn't have a choice," recalls Hall of Fame winger Bert Olmstead, who played in Montreal, Toronto, and Chicago, and is now retired in Calgary. "We had to use CCM with the Canadian teams and Northland with the American ones. Myself, I wanted to use Northland sticks in Toronto – I thought they were better – but they wouldn't let me. I remember Mr. Smythe telling us we had to use a minimum twenty-two-ounce CCM stick. He worried lighter sticks would break if a Northland hit them too hard." Olmstead smiles, recalling the parsimonious Smythe regime in Toronto.

The dominance of CCM and Northland at the NHL level still left plenty of room for other companies in an expanding minor hockey market. CCM, Sherwood, and Victoriaville, among others, became prominent in Quebec and the eastern seaboard. Hespeler remained the big name in Ontario. The department-store catalogue facilitated stick sales right into the 1960s; Eaton's and the Hudson's Bay Company supplied rural areas not served by stores. There was also considerable production under brand names of department stores and hardware chains. Gas companies frequently used sticks as promotional tools to get hockey fans to fill up. Usually – though not always – these sticks were of inferior wood that name-brand manufacturers would rather not have traced back to them.

After the Monarch factory burned down in 1954, the main competition in Ontario for Hespeler was Wally sticks, named for Wallaceburg, Ontario, where they were made. The owner of Wally Enterprises, Jack Lacey, had begun manufacturing corncob pipes at the forks of the Sydenham River. In 1959, Wally Enterprises purchased the old McVean Company in neighbouring Dresden; McVean was the Canadian manufacturer for Hillerich and Bradsby, famed producer of Louisville Slugger baseball bats. (They also produced croquet sets.) All these wood products got Jack Lacey to thinking. "I was on my way back from Toronto and I just got an inspiration," the eighty-eight-year-old retired businessman recalls from his home in London, Ontario. "I said to myself, 'Why don't I get into the hockey-stick business?' I certainly didn't do any market research like they do today. I just knew they broke like crazy, and that'd probably be a good thing to get into."

Lacey pulled off Highway 2 to see Orville Wolfe, the owner of the Ingersoll stick factory. "We talked more or less in circles for a while and then he said, 'Just what the hell do you want?' So I said, 'Do you want to sell your company?' He said he'd think about it.'"

Wolfe thought about it, decided his days as a stick manufacturer were over, then came to see Lacey at the plant in Dresden in August 1959. The two agreed to terms. Wolfe said he'd be in touch as soon as the papers were drawn up. Days passed, and Lacey didn't hear from him. He thought the deal had fallen apart. Then he received a call. "I got word that on his way home, Mr. Wolfe had had a subdural hemorrhage and died, and had been by the side of the road in his car for a day or two." The sale eventually went through with Wolfe's widow finishing the paper work. Lacey – who'd never built a stick in his life – was the proud owner of a stick factory. His bank manager gently asked if he'd taken leave of his senses.

Lacey, who was in the auto-parts business through McVean's, was nonetheless confident. "It's the same as working metal or any other thing. It's a process of removing material, whether wood or brass or copper, and putting things back together again. I was familiar with that kind of operation, so I felt I could handle it." He soon learned that the stick business had its own difficulties. "The problem is your inventories and dating. The minute the season's over [in April], you're building for next year. You're stocking all these sticks and making them to order – whatever your salesmen can get. Well, you don't ship until maybe August or September. And when you ship, the guys want three months' dating [on the bills]. That was a disease in this business, you know – ninety-day terms. You sometimes had your money tied up pretty near all year.

"But I was determined to make it go. The only time I had concerns was at three in the morning sometimes, when I'd look out the window and hope to God those accounts were going to come in by Friday so I could make the payroll. Talk about cash flows . . ."

Among the employees Lacey inherited from Ingersoll Hockey Stick Company was Walter Anderson, who'd alerted Lacey to the first bad shipment of wood and who was by now a foreman and the custom-stick specialist. Ingersoll had developed a sideline selling sticks to Boston Bruins such as Jerry Toppazzini and Real Chevrefils under the Woody Dumart brand. With Ingersoll on board and Anderson as the expert, a stick operation was added to the Louisville Slugger bat line in Dresden. In 1961, the entire operation was moved to its current home in Wallaceburg.

The new operation fought to gain market share in a business dominated by the established names. "They'd say, 'Who are you? You're the new kid on the block. How do I know your sticks are any good? Who uses them?' I'd say the Frenchmen were our greatest competitors, Sher-Wood, CCM, and Victoriaville. They were selling all through here when I started."

In 1966, Hillerich and Bradsby bought out Lacey, who stayed on as general manager until 1971. "I remember they wanted to use the name Louisville Slugger on the sticks. I said, 'Forget it, there's enough goes on in hockey now, you don't need to encourage the guys.' But they were very determined, and the sales manager I had, I guess he wanted to feather his nest. He went along with them. They found out it wasn't a good name for a hockey stick, so they just use Louisville, even today."

At the time Lacey purchased Ingersoll, fibreglass was making inroads as a way to stiffen sticks; laminates and composites were not far off. But Lacey loved – still loves – the properties of white ash. "I remember I was in Austria once, trying to sell hockey sticks, and I had a sample of ash as well as a laminated shaft. They had laminates over there and the guys were giving me a hard time on how much better laminates were. So I said, 'I'll bet you what I have in my pockets that I can break that handle in half a second and you won't break mine.' I put theirs on the chair and the floor. If you kick it right, it just snaps. It hasn't got the give that ash has. Then I put the ash handle there and said, 'Now break it.' Well, all it did was bend and bounce and bend some more. It wouldn't break. That's the difference between the two materials."

Consolidation had come to the stick business. Soon after Lacey sold his shares to Hillerich and Bradsby, the venerable Hespeler St. Mary's operation was swallowed by Cooper Sports, perhaps the best-known name in hockey equipment in Canada. Jack Cooper had started in the leather business in Toronto with Eaton's in 1928, then moved to General Leather Goods. At the height of the Depression the company made shin pads (from 39 cents to $1 a pair) and all-leather hockey gloves ($2 for regular, $4 for pro models). In 1946, Cooper and his partner, Cecil Weeks, started Cooper

Weeks, which became the leading manufacturer of leather protective equipment for hockey and baseball gloves. Many NHL stars wore Cooper Weeks gloves and pads, and the company's products gained a large market share in North America and Europe.

By 1972, Hespeler St. Mary's Wood Products looked ripe for the buying. From gross sales of $500,000 in the early 1960s, the firm was writing $1 million in annual business by the start of the 1970s. But with market consolidation, Hespeler could not survive on sticks alone. So when Cooper Weeks decided to add a hockey-stick maker to complete its product line, the deal was done under the name Cooper Canada. On July 5, 1972, Hespeler St. Mary's Wood Products passed out of the hands of Seagram's after forty-two years at 63 Sheffield Street. Disappearing as well were the famed Hespeler, Mic-Mac, Red Flash, and Green Flash brand names.

Production of wood-based and wood-laminate sticks continued at the Hespeler plant, however, as Cooper Canada fought to keep its market share in the battle with aggressive new challengers from Quebec, the United States, and Europe – all experimenting with new technologies such as fibreglass, laminates, and aluminum. Cooper Canada fought back, making inroads in Europe by forming a partnership in 1982 with the Finnish firm of Diamond Sport Oy. About thirty per cent of the Oy-Cooper sticks were sold to top European stars.

In April 1987, Cooper Canada itself became a target of a buyout by Montreal-based Charan Industries, which paid $37 million for Cooper's assets – including the plant on the bank of the Speed River. The union was short-lived. Within two years, Charan, with financial problems of its own, was looking for a profitable asset to sell. The Cooper division had generated $75 million in sales in 1989; hockey sticks had accounted for about two-thirds of that. It seemed the most likely asset to fetch the money Charan needed to survive. So Charan peddled its Cooper division to Canstar Sport in 1989 (and its baseball-bat division to Irwin Toy). Canstar was heavily into skate making with the Lange, Micron, and Bauer lines, and looking to increase brand-name saturation for those labels. So in 1993 it changed the name on its sticks from Cooper to Bauer. The corporate game of big-fish-eats-small-fish continued in 1999 when Bauer was acquired by the sports equipment giant Nike.

Today, Bauer/Nike Hockey Inc. has its corporate offices in Montreal. Under the present setup, Nike produces composite sticks in California; the Bauer operation, still turning out wooden sticks, remains where it's always been: on the bank of the Speed, just north of Highway 401 amid the urban sprawl of Cambridge, Ontario. "When I started in 1981, there were thirty-six people working here," says John Hicks, assistant plant manager at the Bauer operation. "This factory now employs about 147 people. We run sixteen hours a day – two shifts. Our production for 2000 was about 1.3 million sticks, which includes about 50,000 pro-model sticks. It works out to about 20,000 board feet of wood a month."

About 160 pairs of hands touch a stick at the Hespeler plant – a far cry from Walter Anderson's days, when a dozen employees staffed the plant. Of course, those sticks weren't produced in a place that looks as though NASA engineers were hard at work. "This fellow here," says Hicks, pointing to an employee working a Star Wars contraption, "he's using radio frequencing gluing. That allows you to get a five or six lie on the stick without much variation. There's electric current running from one place to the other. There's water in the glue and electricity shocks the glue, cures it immediately. Every thirty-three seconds he's getting eight sticks."

In every corner of the plant sit computer-driven machines that would have caused old Jacob Hespeler to rub his eyes in disbelief. It almost comes as a relief to see an identifiable machine in the midst of so much high tech. A lonely soul works a band saw amid rows and rows of finished sticks destined for the NHL. "He's cutting the blades for our pro blades," says Hicks. "Our sales reps will send in a blade with a pattern on it. We trace the blade on paper, then band saw each one individually. Nothing is working off jigsaws here, it's all done by hand. So a player can change his pattern and it doesn't affect us a whole lot . . . unlike the graphite blades that can cost up to $5,000 for a construction mould."

When they get a chance, the NHL stars drop by the factory. "Eric Lindros has been here a few times," Hicks says of the injury-plagued Bauer/Nike endorsee. "Ed Belfour and Keith Primeau have been in. Chris Gratton comes in every year as well. The guys who work here get a kick out of it. They love the game and take pride when one of our guys wins the Cup using their sticks. Todd and Rich over there, they talk hockey all day." Hicks smiles, looking around at the controlled confusion around him. "Me, I don't live and breathe hockey. If I did, I'd probably go nuts."

With most NHL stars moving from wood laminates to composite blades and shafts, the days of the Hespeler plant as a stop for NHL stars are coming to an end. The design of their custom product will most likely move to an engineering office somewhere in the silicon belt of the United States. But until the price of those composites moderates, the market for lower-priced wood products will remain vibrant in minor hockey. Who knows? The town of Hespeler may still be turning out hockey sticks the next time God's Zamboni comes rolling through.

CHAPTER 3

THE FRENCH
CONNECTION

We all combed our hair like Maurice Richard, and to keep it
in place we used a kind of glue – a great deal of glue. We
laced our skates like Maurice Richard, we taped our sticks
like Maurice Richard.

Roch Carrier, "The Hockey Sweater", 1979

The first United Empire Loyalists, hungry and scared,
crossed into Lower Canada from the United States with
their worldly possessions in the late 1700s. The names of
the communities they built in the Eastern Townships speak
to the British heritage they were looking to preserve:
Sherbrooke, Drummondville, Lennoxville, Richmond,
Eastman, Waterloo, Victoriaville. Having left everything
behind in their flight northward, the Loyalists needed a way
to carve out a living in their new home. They found the
rolling hills of the Townships blanketed with white pine,

red pine, birch, and sugar maple; soon, forestry, furniture making, maple-syrup production, and pulp and paper became staples of the local economy. The city of Sherbrooke may be the Queen of the Townships, but everyone understood that lumber was king.

The Townships did not remain an Anglo bastion. Francophone workers gravitated to the textile factories in Sherbrooke, the mines in Asbestos and Thetford Mines, the pulp mills on the St. Francis River, the factories of Drummondville. They joined the habitants – the long-time French-speaking farmers of the region – until "*les cantons de l'est*" was a predominantly French-speaking region ruled by the twin forces of the Catholic Church and the English bosses. Quebec nationalism smouldered beneath the surface, but the status quo prevailed for decades. It took the conscription issue during World War II to finally spark the heat into flame.

When compulsory enlistment loomed, some Quebec nationalists advised their followers to resist the "Imperial" war, to practise civil disobedience by avoiding military service. Many French Canadians ignored the message and served gallantly in combat. (The Van Doos, among other regiments, suffered terrible casualties in the invasions of Italy, France, and Holland.) But enough took heed of the pacifist message to cause alarm. The federal Liberal government of Mackenzie King tried a compromise, allowing some recruits to serve in the armed forces with a guarantee they would not be sent overseas. Reserve units – nicknamed Zombies – were soon filled with soldiers committed only to national defence.

In the crisis that followed, Toronto Maple Leafs owner Conn Smythe – himself seriously wounded in action after

D-Day – decried the move, saying raw recruits were being killed in Europe while trained troops remained at home, avoiding combat. In ethnically bifurcated Canada, Smythe was implying that English-speaking boys were dying for peace while French-speaking boys hid out in the woods or in reserve units.

Naturally, hockey provided a forum for debate. Smythe pointed to the Montreal Canadiens. Look at Maurice Richard, he said, the pride of French Quebec. If he was healthy enough to score fifty goals in 1944, why wasn't he healthy enough to serve? (Richard was declared unfit because of a severely broken leg suffered in 1942–43.) Meanwhile, Maple Leaf personnel, from the owner down to the trainer, were signing up. (Ignored by Smythe was the fact that the Habs' English-speaking goalie, Bill Durnan, also missed the war because the club had secured him a war-related industry job.)

Prime Minister King was able to smooth the waters before they erupted into civil strife, but the "Quiet Revolution" had taken on a life. When longtime Quebec premier Maurice Duplessis died in 1959, the traditional culture of Anglo patronage and union-busting politics died with him. A new generation became firmly entrenched in Quebec City under the slogan "*Maître chez nous.*" English cultural and linguistic superiority in the province was effectively dead after 200 years of hegemony. Within ten years, the province had its first politically inspired kidnapping and murder; within twenty, it was voting on potential separation from Canada.

In this mix of French-Canadian cultural frustration, a young hardware clerk in Sherbrooke, Quebec, cast off linguistic stereotypes to build the greatest stick-making operation in the world. Leo Drolet was not thinking about Quebec pride in 1949 when he borrowed $500 from his parents and his father-in-law to plough into Sherbrooke Woodcraft Products. He was simply looking for a sideline to supplement his income from Dawson Auto Parts, the hardware store where he worked. But listen to him describe Sher-Wood's humble beginnings, and you hear the larger themes of the day.

"In Quebec in those days," he told author Gilles Pelchat, "no one had confidence in the products we made here. They didn't want to lose their money, and they preferred to buy in Ontario or anywhere else. When you said it was made in Quebec, it wouldn't sell. It's only in Ontario it seemed where they have lots of money, that they can produce anything of quality."

Apart from the questionable reputation of Quebec products, Drolet's fledgling company was also up against a shaky market for sticks in the austere economy of post-war Quebec. There simply wasn't a lot of money to spend in most households, particularly off the island of Montreal. Much of the stick buying was done through the local clubs; kids in the street typically used home-fashioned sticks. Trying to buy sticks in bulk from a hardware store or garage was largely unheard of in the days following the war. But Leo Drolet loved a challenge.

In 1949, the thirty-eight-year old Drolet was responsible for buying and selling the sporting goods at Dawson's. "We bought mostly from Hespeler," he recalls. "It was hard to get sticks from Hespeler during the war and even after." He also doubled as middleman for Sherbrooke Wood Products, a local stick factory, peddling their products around the area in summer. When the manufacturer, Yvan Dugre, decided to sell directly to his suppliers – cutting Drolet out – Leo resolved to make sticks himself.

He knew precious little about the manufacturing side of the business, so he looked at the operations of CCM in nearby St. Jean d'Iberville and his former clients at Sherbrooke Wood Products. "I knew CCM made their sticks out of ash and their blades out of elm, but that was about it. I learned fast, however – for example, the ash that grows in the swamps around here is black; it's worthless. There are different textures of ash. You want the ash that comes from the higher ground."

With $10,000 he'd borrowed from family, friends, and the bank, Drolet turned his newly acquired knowledge to making sticks at Sherbrooke Woodcraft Products (not to be confused with Sherbrooke Wood Products). The ambitious Drolet was still balancing his new stick company with working at Dawson's – often putting in twenty-hour days. (His first invoice in 1949 for $532.87 to Dawson Auto Parts he keeps framed behind his desk.) He soon learned that the success of his Sher-Wood business would rely on hard work and good suppliers. It was not unusual for him to lose $500 or even $1,000 on a shipment of bad wood from an untrustworthy shipper. But he learned, and he developed a network.

His first suppliers were from local towns such as Scotstown, Bromont, and Cowansville; soon he was scouting the northeastern United States. "I looked for logs in New Hampshire and Maine – mostly ash. When we went to Ontario, it was to buy elm. On the weekend I'd hit the road with 'Ti-Gilles' Lemire, who'd go with me. He worked as a driver, mechanic, a jack of all trades. He'd drive the car at night while I slept in the back. In the morning, I'd go look at wood and he'd sleep in the car. Then we'd come home in the evening. That way we didn't waste time."

While the fledgling outfit benefited from its proximity to one of the world's top stick-buying markets, the riches of Montreal also attracted competitors. Something like forty-two companies – including Cho-Wood in St. Jean, Super Strong in Valleyfield, Hard Wood in Quebec City, and Victoriaville in that city – were all competing in the same Montreal–Quebec City marketplace. The companies that would prosper had to look beyond Quebec for outlets and consumers. Drolet established strong regional representatives to conquer the lucrative Ontario and western Canadian markets. He also established a presence in the northeastern United States, selling American ash back to Americans under a French-Canadian imprimatur.

With a toehold in the market, Drolet began thinking six months or a year ahead in the buying/manufacturing cycle. He'd bring out his new model in short supply, make it hard to obtain, and convince skeptical buyers it was a hot seller. The next season they'd order more of that model to be sure that they had enough to meet "demand." And consumers would buy extra sticks to make sure they had enough for the season.

Still, there were setbacks when shipments didn't arrive or when the sticks broke too easily. "One Sunday," remembers longtime employee Jean-Louis Coté, "there was an unhappy client who approached Mme. Drolet, looking for Leo. He'd been looking everywhere for him. She told him he could find him in church. So the client waited outside till the end of the mass. When he saw Leo come out, he dropped all his broken hockey sticks at the feet of M. Drolet. That's pretty humiliating, isn't it?"

Despite the setbacks, the business grew, from $46,900 in sales in 1949 to $230,700 in 1955 to $1.739 million in 1969. Drolet had his sales staff in Canada and the United States work every rink, sporting goods store, and hardware outlet. He expanded the distribution of Sher-Wood to Europe and developed a reputation as a man not to be crossed. One friend remembers a rival picking up a Sher-Wood stick and breaking it in front of delegates at the annual Canadian Sporting Goods Association convention. The competitor defiantly brandished the broken stick in front of other delegates. An incensed Drolet approached him and said something quiet and terse. The rival quickly dropped the stick and walked away. There would be no more public destruction of Leo Drolet's sticks.

Drolet incorporated the latest technological innovations into his sticks. Sometimes it took a legal challenge to do so. Before he could bring out his first fibreglass-reinforced stick blades in 1957, he had to go to court against the Mailhot brothers, who ran Victoriaville sticks. The Mailhots had obtained a patent for fibreglassing the blades of sticks to make them stronger. They wanted Sher-Wood prohibited from bringing out a similar stick, but Drolet proved he had been fibreglassing blades for two years before the patent was granted to Victoriaville. This small legal triumph would have major repercussions when hockey players grew bigger and stronger and demanded stiffer sticks. (Drolet eventually had a falling-out with André Michaud – whose company, Lead-Flex, had helped Sher-Wood develop its fibreglassing techniques. Michaud left that company to help start up rival Canadien sticks.)

By the time the NHL expanded from six to twelve teams in 1967, the Sher-Wood plant was among the busiest in the business. But to meet the demands of an expanding market, more capital was needed than Drolet could raise himself. He made plans to sell his business to Adirondack Industries, a branch of the American company Rowan Industries. Then, as so often in the tumultuous history of the business, fire intervened. On the evening of July 16, a three-alarm blaze levelled the Sher-Wood plant, causing $2 million in damage. When the stacked pallets of wood, gallons of solvents, and vats of glues had finally burned themselves out, the city's fire chief called it the worst fire in the city in decades.

"It was the start of the holidays," Leo Drolet told Pelchat. "The whole family was with me at the lake. I left here about midnight with Michel and Denis. When we reached the out-skirts of Lennoxville [the next town], we could already see the flames. As I drove, I had a lot to think about [such as] how am I going to continue?" Drolet suspected arson, but nothing was proven. The factory was insured for only about a quarter of its value. To make matters worse, Drolet's health suddenly deteriorated, putting the future of Sher-Wood in doubt. He underwent surgery – even as the fire marshals were still picking through the wreckage of his plant.

But Leo Drolet was a fighter. *"Moi, j'ai la tête dure,"* he told author Pelchat – "I'm hard-headed." Within months of his surgery, he'd found a deserted textile factory overlooking the Magog River in Sherbrooke's industrial section. After purchasing it, he relaunched the firm (a grateful city later renamed the bordering street rue Sherwood) and within nine months had an agreement on the sale of the company to Adirondack Industries that would let him run the business with needed capital input. Three years later, Sher-Wood was enjoying its best year ever.

⌣

During the 1950s and 1960s, the white-ash sticks seen by viewers of "Hockey Night in Canada" were unadorned with jazzy graphics or glaring paint jobs. Regional preferences, strong sales forces, and strategic price points were far more important than endorsements by NHL players in fuelling the retail market. But soon, increased television exposure, the continuing expansion of the NHL, the creation of the World Hockey Association in 1972, and the advent of sports marketing groups such as Mark McCormack's International Management Group all conspired to put a greater emphasis on having top players seen using a manufacturer's product.

Hockey wasn't the only part of Canadian society that was changing. Marshall McLuhan's academic haunts could not have been farther removed from the cloistered, jock world of the dressing room, but his insistence that the medium is the message helped lead professional hockey to a deeper understanding of the importance of image and of marketing. Gradually, the conservative owners of teams found themselves opting for jazzier uniforms (remember the white skates of the California Golden Seals?), snazzier game presentations (scoreboards around the NHL went from telling the time to telling fans when to cheer), and branded equipment.

The stick became a walking advertisement almost by accident: Montreal's star goalie Ken Dryden was famous for propping his chin on his Sher-Wood goal stick during lulls in the action. When this casual pose attracted the attention of TV cameras, Sher-Wood executive Georges Guilbault suggested increasing the size of the lettering on the stick tenfold. Soon the branding on all sticks was jumbo-sized. If "Hockey Night in Canada" was going to provide a billboard, Sher-Wood was going to use it. (Dryden, now president of the Maple Leafs, was unaware of his role in the branding of sticks until it was mentioned to him in late 2000.) Today, product names are bannered across any visible piece of equipment on a player (as well as on the boards, the clock, and the ice), and the NHL charges a tidy fee for the privilege.

Leo Drolet – having been joined in the business by sons Michel and Denis – understood that player endorsements could affect stick retailing. Better yet, it could affect pricing; Sher-Wood sticks were all the more attractive when handled by stars. With NHL players who'd become TV stars as its sales force, Sher-Wood pushed the price for its product. In the 1960s, five dollars was the psychological barrier for a top stick; by the mid-1970s, endorsement appeal had helped raise that to $10, then $15, then $25 for a wood stick.

Drolet was helped by changes at the NHL level. The disintegration of the CCM and Northland domination of NHL sticks in the 1960s took only a few years. Victoriaville was among the first companies to break the NHL barrier, thanks

Ken Dryden's classic resting pose, which the cameras loved,
prompted Sher-Wood to treat his goalie stick as a kind of
television billboard

to francophone players such as Serge Savard and Jean Beliveau, the pride of Victoriaville. "In the 1950s, we used only CCM sticks," Beliveau recalled. "I had gone to school with the Mailhot brothers, who started Victoriaville. One day in the '60s they came to practice with a few sticks, and I tried them. Some of the blades went flying all over the place. So they went back and worked on it and came up with a very good stick. After that, I played with them to the end of my career." At the peak of its NHL popularity, Victoriaville also boasted Bobby Orr, Rod Gilbert, Frank Mahovlich, and Larry Robinson, as well as goalies such as Rogatien Vachon and Chico Resch.

Sher-Wood was close behind, having added Bobby Clarke and Guy Lafleur to its Dryden-led stable of stars. By 1970, Leo Drolet had more than 200 pros under contract. Sher-Wood's customized service – it was the first to offer made-to-measure models to the stars – gave it a distinct advantage for a time. But players still had to be won over, and it fell to Michel Drolet, Leo's eldest son, to do the wooing. He recalls the frustration of trying to convert Bruins star Phil Esposito to the Sher-Wood product. When numerous visits, proto-types, and attempts at flattery failed, Drolet found himself outside the Bruins' dressing room, disconsolate. Ted Green, the Bruins' tough defenceman, called him over. "Make me some sticks and I'll use them," said Green. "You're wasting your time with Phil. If I use your sticks, other players on the Bruins will do the same."

Drolet did, and within a year fifteen Bruins players were using Sher-Wood. "That's when I understood that it's not always the stars you have to approach," said Michel Drolet.

"There are born leaders [who aren't necessarily stars]. If a company rep can get their ear about his products, you'll soon see other players come over as well."

Georges Guilbault, Sher-Wood's longtime marketing guru, recalls that Northland signed his client Bobby Clarke away from Sher-Wood one September at training camp. A perturbed Guilbault caught up with the Philadelphia captain just as he was about to pose for photos with his new friends at Northland – former Chicago players Moose Vasko and Ken Wharram. While the cameraman set up lights, Guilbault pulled Clarke aside to ask why he'd changed his mind. Clarke explained that the Northland people had promised his unemployed brother a job as a Northland rep in western Canada. Guilbault immediately matched the offer; Clarke returned to tell Vasko and Wharram the Northland deal was off.

Now it was the former players who were miffed. They confronted the Sher-Wood executive. "Look," Guilbault said, "you're not going to steal my players. You've got to learn something in this business. That guy there is my guy. I won't steal your guys, don't steal mine."

Of course, Guilbault was still obliged to find a job for Clarke's brother in the west. The problem was that Sher-Wood had no jobs in the west. As Guilbault was steeling himself to tell Clarke he couldn't make good on his promise, Clarke phoned to say his brother had found a job – he didn't need a position with Sher-Wood after all. Guilbault breathed a huge sigh of relief, having never disclosed his dilemma to Clarke.

Of course, Sher-Wood was not above trying to lure a

player on the stick's merits, as Guilbault proved in wooing Lafleur, the NHL's greatest star at that time. The Canadiens' brilliant right winger was under contract to KOHO, the Finnish company, when Guilbault persuaded Canadiens trainer Pierre Meilleur to let him show Lafleur his wares at practice. An excited Guilbault had painstakingly built Sher-Wood models that matched the specs on Lafleur's KOHO sticks. He watched in dismay as, one after the other, Lafleur broke his precious models like match sticks. Back to the drawing board.

The next week, Guilbault returned to the Forum with improved sticks. A cranky Lafleur had been in a slump and was not predisposed to more testing. Guilbault persisted; Lafleur resisted, reminding the Sher-Wood rep of how easily he'd ruined the previous batch. In response, Guilbault took two of Lafleur's prepared game sticks and broke them against a pillar to show Lafleur that his KOHOs were not infallible, either. Lafleur was angry, but accepted the reworked Sher-Woods for a game test.

Lafleur began that night's game using his KOHO. When it broke, he had Meilleur pull the Sher-Wood off his stick rack. On his first shift, he scored. Later that night he added two more goals: a hat-trick the first time he used Sher-Woods. Not long afterwards, he became a Sher-Wood poster boy.

As more firms entered the market, the competition for players became fierce. André Michaud – who had started up Canadien Hockey Sticks with Marcel Goupil and Gaston Ruel after leaving Drolet's employ – was soon in the hunt. And the Scandinavian invasion of KOHO, Jofa, and Titan was also at hand. Before long, the European companies would command a third of the global stick market. The old way of doing business was dying.

A stick in the Original Six era weighed as much as a kilogram. By the 1970s, players wanted lighter models that didn't sacrifice strength or durability. A stick with less weight produces a faster shot by speeding up the blade at impact. A player firing a 65-mph slapshot with, say, a 500-gram stick will increase the speed of that shot by ten per cent, to more than 71 mph, if the stick is reduced to 413 grams. In the NHL, that can easily be the difference between a goal and a save.

The European companies had been lightening the stick for years by the time Canadian companies such as Sher-Wood began slicing weight off their models. But when Sher-Wood first tried to make sticks lighter and more responsive, players snapped them like balsa wood. "*Fort comme un boeuf*," marvelled Guilbault of Lafleur's ability to break his best sticks. "Strong as a bull." Across the NHL, the scene was repeating itself. How, then, to reduce the mass of the traditional wood stick without sacrificing strength or stiffness?

For almost twenty years manufacturers had been wrapping fibreglass around the blade. What if you applied fibreglass to the shaft as well? Fibreglass had many applications before hockey discovered it, of course, and the qualities that made it ideal for reinforcing everything from auto parts to diving boards became evident when sheets of fibreglass cloth were wrapped around the shaft and then coated with resin.

Weight could be removed from the shaft without giving up durability. Presto: stronger, lighter sticks.

Fibreglass also allowed the use of less expensive woods, such as aspen. Aspen is light (twenty-five pounds per cubic foot) compared to white ash (forty-one pounds), but not strong enough on its own to withstand the torque of an NHL slapshot. As Sher-Wood and Canadien discovered, aspen reinforced with fibreglass had both strength and lightness. And because aspen was a fast-growing wood, it lowered production costs as well.

"Canadien out of Drummondville was really revolutionary in manufacturing wood fibreglass sticks," recalls Steve Davies, who first made his mark as a jobber, or distributor, of sticks with International Stick Company in Toronto. "They came out with the first moulded fibreglass shaft, putting fibreglass on a wood core. Then Sher-Wood followed with their lamination version of a wood core, and that started the era of stiffer, more durable, more expensive sticks."

"I remember in the beginning of the 1970s when I was playing hockey here in Drummondville," recalls Jacques Chasson, a longtime employee of Canadien. "This company started with fibreglass cloth. From there we went to moulded fibreglass. Sher-Wood started with fibreglass laminates. That was the major evolution in the stick. Aspen core with a fibreglass shaft – or a mixture of aspen and birch. Us and Sher-Wood. The other companies were still using solid hardwood." Eventually, paper birch (also known as white or northern birch) replaced aspen as the core wood for Canadien and Sher-Wood shafts. Its combination of density, weight, and flexibility – and its ready availability in the Quebec market – won over the manufacturers. It also had good shock resistance.

"The wood is only a third of the stick's stiffness," points out Marc Vosteen, who works with Chasson at the Canadien factory off Highway 20 in Drummondville. "The rest [of the stiffness] is put on using carbon or fibreglass. That is every-body's Kentucky Fried Chicken secret recipe. All the com-panies have their own recipe. The carbon is not the secret. The fibreglass is not the secret. It's the recipe of what holds the carbon and fibreglass to the shaft."

To meet its technological demands, Sher-Wood in 1976 created InGlas, a company responsible for refining the fibreglassing process. As Sher-Wood's market share grew, the patents obtained for its processes proved highly profitable and in 1994 allowed the Drolets to reacquire Sher-Wood from its American owners. InGlas also branched out into other profitable enterprises for Sher-Wood; for example, InGlas has the licence to produce the official pucks for the NHL.

Others in the hockey world strove to stay on top of the technology as well. The search was on for more effective resins and carbons and fibreglass. "We have engineers who make up recipes to hold the carbon on the stick," says Vosteen. "We've got refrigerators to keep the chemicals, everything temperature controlled. This is almost like NASA." At the old Hespeler factory, meanwhile, the Bauer/ Nike folks discovered that the way to keep up with the Drolets was to look overseas. "To this day, we buy our veneer to laminate our sticks from Finland," says John Hicks. "It's aircraft veneer, and Finland's the only place in the world where it's made."

⌐——

Ah, Finland. Much of the hockey-stick evolution in the 1970s had its origins in the Scandinavian nation of 5 million souls tucked up against what was then the USSR. Without any preconceived ideas of how to make sticks, they experimented freely. Using technology borrowed from skiing, the Finns perfected the lighter, stronger stick. At the same time that Canada's markets were opening to the consumer-friendly innovations of Japanese automobiles, German audio equipment, and Swedish furniture, the stick industry also surrendered market share to a European invader.

"In Finland, they revolutionized the art of hockey-stick making," recalls Carl Brewer, the iconoclastic, four-time NHL All-Star with the Toronto Maple Leafs, St. Louis Blues, and Detroit Red Wings. Sitting on a sofa in the Toronto home of his friend Sue Foster, just back from one of their sojourns to France, Brewer recalls the quixotic journey through the hockey world that took him to Helsinki in 1968. Fed up with the NHL's closed-shop atmosphere after eight seasons under the lash of Punch Imlach in Toronto, Brewer played for Canada's national team in 1967. That experience in the world of international hockey led him to accept an assignment as a player with HFK Helsinki for the 1968–69 season. Brewer delighted in the free-flowing style of European hockey – and the beauty of Finnish sticks.

"The KOHO stick was made with five pieces of ash laminated together to form the handle. In Canada, we used just a single piece of ash in the shaft at that time. The design was exceptional and the graphics on the sticks were very powerful. The stick had an incredible feel to it – not very heavy, a good balance from the handle to the blade, and the proper stiffness for me. "

For a player brought up on the heavy ash sticks produced by Canadian companies, Brewer found the KOHO and Montreal Surprise models a revelation. It was a bit like comparing the first, cumbersome laptop computers to today's lightweight models. Before he left Finland in 1969 to return to the NHL, Brewer was not only a convert to playing with Finnish sticks, he was importing them into Canada as well.

How the Finns lightened the stick is a lesson in ingenuity. Finland is heavily forested, but its commercial stands generally lie too far north for the growth of hardwoods comparable to those in Canadian and northern American forests. Wood that grows in Finland's northern climate tends to be dense and strong, but too heavy for use in sticks. North American wood, by comparison, tends to grow in a climate cold enough to produce strong fibres but not so frigid as to make those fibres too heavy and inflexible. If the Finns had used their wood and North American methods to make sticks, they'd have turned out small logs.

To get lightness, flexibility, and strength in cross-country skis, Finnish manufacturers cut the plentiful birch into thin strips, then glued the strips together to produce a multi-ply "wafer" or "sandwich" of woods. Finnish stick manufacturers began making blades the same way, bonding thin strips of birch with epoxy and fibreglass to make a blade that was lighter and more consistent than the one-piece ash blade in Canada. This "stack and split" method promotes strength and resists splitting and cracking. To further lighten sticks, manufacturers perforated the wood and hollowed out the shaft without jeopardizing its stiffness or strength. In later incarnations, the laminated blade would be sealed with plastic coating or Kevlar, used in bulletproof clothing. This multi-ply technology revolutionized the manufacture of sticks in the late 1960s and early '70s.

The strength of Canadian sticks had always derived from the fibres of the white ash; the strength of Finnish sticks lay in the glues and laminates that held the wood plies together. Using this ply approach, manufacturers could also utilize less-than-perfect wood, hollow out the shaft, and adjust veneers to improve shock absorbency. In some models, as many as fifty-two layers of wood were bonded with fifty-one layers of glue; in others, plywood was used. Experience showed fourteen or twenty-one plies of birch or ash worked best.

"I started playing with a KOHO when I was thirteen years old," recalls Teemu Selanne, perhaps the greatest Finnish player in history (Jari Kurri fans might argue the point). "The competition was hard, there were two or three different companies, so everybody had to pay attention. I still use pretty much the same stick. They've been doing it for such a long time that they take pride in doing a real good job."

Carl Brewer was introduced to the men who pioneered these techniques. Rauli Virtanen had begun to manufacture sticks under the trade name Black Hawk in 1961; four years later, he merged his operation with Kohotuote-oy, run by Kari Yro. Their first year together, they made 25,000 sticks in their factory in Forsa. Eight years later, when the factory was sold, they were producing as many as 10,000 KOHO sticks a day.

"Kari was the prime designer, builder, and architect of things with KOHO," recalls Brewer. "But they were both incredibly creative, talented guys. So I made arrangements with them for some sample sticks to be sent over to Canada."

About the time he met the KOHO people, Brewer was also introduced to Kalevi Numminen, one of the great names in Finnish hockey as both player and coach (and the father of Teppo Numminen of the Phoenix Coyotes). Numminen produced a stick known as the Montreal Surprise in Tampere. "I tended to use the Montreal Surprise," Brewer says. "They were very light, and could be stiff-handled. They were fine sticks, and they changed everything in the marketplace." After turning down Numminen's request to coach in Finland, Brewer obtained samples to bring back to Canada where, now free of obligation to the Maple Leafs, he planned an NHL comeback with Detroit.

KOHO and Montreal Surprise were not the only companies creating sticks that would change the market. Karhu, a Finnish ski manufacturer, was using its technology to produce Titan sticks. Owner Anti Tittola, a former Olympic ski champion, designed fibreglass and wood skis and decided to construct a stick from the remnants of a ski. The initial results were less than spectacular, says George Kaz, who later marketed Titan, KOHO, and Canadien sticks. "Karhu was a ski company, first and foremost. According to players who used them when they first came over from Finland, they were pieces of junk."

The former Islander Mike Bossy, Titan's first NHL poster
boy and one of the most prolific goal scorers in NHL history,
concurs. "I put up with a lot when I first started. But I'd
signed with them, so I stuck it out." Titan kept working on
the marriage of plastics and wood, and became the first
company to employ ABS (acrylonitrile butadiene styrene), a
highly impact-resistant plastic first employed to connect
blade and shaft and now universally used in stick blades. By
the mid-'80s, Titan sticks were a force in the NHL market.
"An exceptionally fine stick," Brewer says of the Titan.

Even as they sought to conquer the Canadian market, the
Finns left no doubt where their inspiration lay: Finnish
brands included names such as Sherbrooke, Canadian, and
Toronto. "All it was," says Kaz, "was a way to develop a spot
in the Canadian marketplace. 'Let's name a stick Canadian.'
And away they went."

Back in North America with the Red Wings in 1969–70,
Brewer turned heads with his Finnish sticks and his
European-influenced play. After four seasons away from
the NHL, he was again voted to the All-Star team. "A funny
story," he chuckles. "We played in Montreal late in that
season. We never used to win in Montreal in those days. But
in the last minute I directed a shot toward the net. I believe
all goals are basically flukes – and I got lucky. This one went
in and we won 6–5, I believe. So the Red Wings surprised the
Canadiens by winning at the Forum. And the stick I used to
win the game was called . . . the Montreal Surprise."

Brewer's Detroit teammates soon adopted the Finnish
sticks he was using. When Garry Unger was dealt from the
Wings to St. Louis, he took the KOHO model with him. With

its snappy graphics, sharp colours, surprising lightness, and multi-ply handle, it captured the market's fancy. "In those days, players weren't paid to use a stick," recalls Brewer. "They just played with the stick they liked. Players liked the looks and the feel of the KOHO, and it wasn't difficult to convince them to use it. It became popular very quickly."

KOHO also changed the market in another way. "When we went to the marketplace with them in 1968," recalls Brewer, "people said, 'You're nuts, no hockey stick will retail for five dollars.' Well, they were wrong. People did pay five bucks for a KOHO, and more. And we could never satisfy the demand."

From storing a few models in his Toronto garage, Brewer was soon using his parents' garage, then a friend's basement, to house the sticks. "We were bringing in container loads. Each container would be roughly 20,000 sticks and we'd increase the number of containers each year. The orders got bigger and bigger." So big, in fact, that when Brewer had a falling-out with Detroit management, he became a stick distributor. The explanation for his retirement in *Total Hockey* is succinct: "Left Detroit training camp Sept. 4, 1970, to concentrate on job with KOHO stick company."

Brewer's "boutique" stick business expanded quickly in the early 1970s. But behind the scenes things were not going smoothly. After KOHO ran into financial problems, its factory in Forsa was sold in 1973. Rauli Virtanen, the co-founder, moved to Long Island to supervise stick production for the NHL. For the next five years, materials were sent to KOHO in New York to be assembled for pro players. There were other changes as well. "You find that loyalties don't last too long in business," Brewer says cryptically. A sly smile creeps across his face. "They were making changes, and I was one of the changes they made. I lasted in the stick business till 1976. And then, it seems, I got out of the stick business."

⌐

About the time Brewer left the importing business, consolidation again became the order of the day; Canadian and Finnish companies merged to become more competitive. In 1976, Karhu transferred its Titan stick technology to Cowansville, Quebec, where it also made cross-country skis. In 1980 KOHO purchased the Canadien stick operation started in Drummondville by André Michaud and others from the ashes of the Sher-Wood fire. Karhu/Titan then swallowed up the holding company for KOHO and Canadien in 1986. Finally, in 2000, CCM bought the entire KOHO/Titan/Canadien family of sticks, making Drummondville the centre of operations under the umbrella name of The Hockey Corporation. The notion of a "Canadian" or "Finnish" stick company was over.

Global forces were being felt in the Canadian hockey world, and it wasn't just the Finns who got in on the act. Georges Guilbault of Sher-Wood remembers that, in the 1970s, "the Japanese began buying up all the best Canadian and American ash and shipping it to San Diego. They'd transfer it to processing boats offshore. They'd make it into plywood right on the boat and sell it back into the North American market." These aggressive business practices, combined with the laminates from Finland, effectively ended the single-piece ash shaft created in the workshops of Hespeler Wood products fifty years earlier.

The stick that began the 1970s as a two- or three-piece wood creation with some fibreglass tape on the blade had morphed into something quite different by the end of the decade. As the '80s began, Sher-Wood and Canadien/KOHO were battling Titan to see who could find a superior method of applying fibreglass to the shaft, who could taper the shaft for a better grip, and who could build the best blades using laminates and plastic.

For a time, the companies used a wood or laminate core with a fibreglass application on top. Then a fibreglass core, with wood enclosing it, became the rage. Manufacturers tried a wood core wrapped in fibreglass and covered in another layer of wood. They began weaving fibreglass and carbon compounds around the shaft to reinforce the stick. There seemed no end to the innovation. The KOHO 221 was met by the Sher-Wood 5030 and the Ultralight 8001 from Canadien. Titan launched the TPM 2020, Victoriaville the Ultra Vic, and Torspo (another Finnish company) brought forth the Pro 500.

The frantic innovation brought the occasional hiccup. When Sher-Wood started making laminated handles, they weren't sure the glues holding the plies together would work. "At one point, I sold sticks to the entire Western Canada Junior League," recalls Guilbault. "We sent them out there in a boxcar, and they froze on the way. The glue went brittle. When the players started using them, they broke like candles. The shipment was useless."

Refinements were made to the glue recipe, and laminated

sticks became standard. Better machines and lamination techniques were also taking the guesswork out of grading wood. Stick makers were able to use more of the wood purchased from mills. "The gurus of the business, a guy like Leo Drolet, for instance, he would buy a flatbed trailer truck of ash and have to determine by eye how many number 1 shafts versus number 2 shafts versus number 3 shafts there are in the load," says Steve Davies. "And that's impossible to do. Obviously the number 1s give you the highest prices, and usually they're only ten per cent of the load. The number 3s are very whippy, they're not very functional, so you've got to use them for Junior handles or tomato stakes. The advent of lamination to the wood business meant that you could prefab a stick that had consistent characteristics of weight and stiffness. You could use all the woods you'd ever want and glue them together – the real strength was in the lamination, not the raw material."

The increasingly sophisticated production at Sher-Wood was matched by down-home marketing innovations. Looking at a GM vehicle bought for him by Leo Drolet, Guilbault noticed the inscription "Body by Fisher" on the frame. "I thought it was an interesting marketing idea that personalized the quality of the product," Guilbault recalled. So he took a proposal to Leo Drolet. Why not put the handwritten inscription "Made by Leo Drolet" on their sticks to signify their quality and sophisticated technology? At first, the Sher-Wood founder resisted, saying he found it pretentious. But Guilbault persisted, and Drolet relented. Today, it's a matter of corporate pride that "Made by Leo Drolet" appears on all the company's sticks.

Not all the technological problems created by fibreglass required space-age solutions. The application of fibreglass to the shaft gave a stick an unhealthy, milky, yellow colour – hardly conducive to sales. Sticks had always been a healthy brown or tan shade with the graphics stencilled or screened on top. Consumers could see how good the wood was in the shaft. But repeated experiments failed to replace the jaundiced look with the natural healthy colour of the wood. The people at Canadien discovered they could colour the fibreglass and turn it white. Would the market buy a white stick, or would it be laughed at? As so often, consumers were ahead of the producers. Canadien's white shafts became the rage among young players.

At Titan in Cowansville, marketers learned how critical this sort of marketing flash had become. With sales of Titan mushrooming because of the endorsements of the young stars Bossy and Gretzky, Titan was running low on stocks of top-grade wood. The only wood available contained knots and blemishes. In desperation, the Karhu head office said, "Slap some paint on them – we'll clear them out and see what happens."

Titan shipped a white stick with red lettering and a red stick with white lettering – knots and all. Company officials were prepared for the worst, perhaps even a rude exit from the industry. Instead, endorsed by Bossy and Gretzky, these coloured sticks became a phenomenon. Nobody noticed the lousy wood, only the colours. Before long sticks were being marketed in a rainbow of colours.

The future of the industry seemed clear – laminates, fibreglass, plastics, and marketing pizzazz – though not everyone felt that wood was dead. Even the advent of aluminum sticks in the early 1980s left Sher-Wood's Guilbault, a veteran of the business, unimpressed. "I don't believe that's the real future of sticks," he said in 1989. "The first criterion for a good stick is feel. You can go with plastic skates, sure, but the hands are more sensitive than the feet. The stick is a more sensitive piece of equipment. Nothing will ever replace the original wood."

Famous last words.

CHAPTER 4

THE FACTORY FLOOR

Advertising may be described as the science of arresting
human intelligence long enough to get money from it.

Stephen Leacock, "The Perfect Salesman," 1924

The idea of using aluminum in sticks was not new. During
World War II, some stick manufacturers had trouble sourcing wood and used aluminum instead. But those pioneer
models were cold, unresponsive, and quickly abandoned
with the return of peace. In 1980, Easton – an American
baseball-bat manufacturer – decided to apply the technology
it was using in bats to the shaft of hockey sticks. The ration-
ale was as it had been in baseball. Aluminum is light and malleable, and bauxite, from which aluminum is made, is
abundant. Wood stocks were declining, prices were up, and
sticks – like bats – broke too often. Aluminum bats had
quickly become standard everywhere but in the major leagues

(which feared the livelier bats would upset the sport's competitive balance between hitters and pitchers). It was the same scenario in tennis, right into the pro ranks. American Jimmy Connors conquered the tennis world using a Wilson metal racket that brought overwhelming power to what had been a serve-and-volley game. Within a few years, wooden rackets and presses were left to gather dust in the attic.

Easton believed the same would happen in hockey once parents got the price-conscious message and players got over their superstitions. After all, you had a seemingly unbreakable shaft to go with an easily insertable ash or laminated blade. "It does cost $49," said Brian Urman of CCM in a 1984 issue of *The Hockey News*. "But the shaft could last an entire season. With the aluminum stick, you only have to replace the blade, which is about $9." For professional players, the controlled manufacturing process meant that exact specifications could be replicated. That was a serious consideration for manufacturers, who saw as many as seventy-five per cent of their sticks rejected by finicky players.

But there were problems translating the technology. "In hockey, you need the spring in the stick," says Marc Vosteen of The Hockey Company. "In baseball, they don't need spring. It's just the pure impact of bat on ball. It's the whip you want in hockey. Aluminum has too much vertical stiffness to give you the whip you get in a wood stick." As well, the first aluminum sticks tended to ring and vibrate in players' hands. There was a problem with warpage (even today, an NHLer might warp two or three shafts a game). And the sticks were cold to the touch – not exactly a selling point to anyone using aluminum outdoors.

Similar complaints about aluminum products had arisen in other sports. In tennis, aluminum had made possible unprecedented power, but at the expense of the control associated with wood. While a pro like Jimmy Connors made aluminum work brilliantly, the recreational player felt like he had a frying pan in his hands. Within months of Connors' vaulting to world supremacy using his Wilson racket, designers were introducing graphite compounds, aiming for the perfect combination of aluminum's power and wood's more sensitive feel.

In hockey, a few top names – Hall of Fame defenceman Brad Park, for one – championed the new technology in the early '80s. Park used an Easton-built stick distributed by Christian Brothers for almost eighteen months in practice before the NHL would allow it in games. "It's something you're going to see a lot more of in the future," he told *The Hockey News* in 1982. "You have a stick that has the same weight all the time, the same stiffness, the same feel. And on top of that, it's less expensive. It's going to be great for the kids."

Dampeners were added to the blade, to reduce the ringing sensation, and various oval-type shafts were developed, to decrease the "bees-in-the-hands" sensation from mishit slapshots. Gradually, the aluminum sticks gained a toehold in the market. Easton licensed both Christian Brothers in Minnesota and Canadien in Quebec to market the Easton 7001 for several years. In the mid-1980s, however, the company decided to market its sticks directly. And what better way to obtain market share than to buy the affections of hockey's greatest offensive machine?

At the time, Wayne Gretzky was still using the Titan TPM 2020, an Ultra glass and wood product he'd helped popularize. Along with Bossy, Michel Goulet, Lanny McDonald, and Rick Vaive, Gretzky had made Titan/KOHO/Canadien a force. Easton was looking to challenge them and sought to wrest the Great One away from its competitor by waving serious bucks.

"The bottom line was, Easton was prepared to pay Gretzky substantial six figures," recalls George Kaz, with Titan at the time. "We were prepared to pay six figures, but not what Easton was willing to pay. Plus, we had Mario Lemieux. Mario's agent, Tom Reich, said, 'If Gretzky is Hertz, then we're a damn good Avis. We can't be all that far off what Gretzky is getting.' And we said, if we start handing out that kind of money to Gretzky and Lemieux, that just about blows the budget."

In the end, Titan let Gretzky go to Easton and concentrated on Lemieux and a promising junior named Eric Lindros. It didn't hurt that Gretzky continued wearing equipment from Titan's sister company, Jofa. "So Wayne went and basically put Easton on the market with the manufacturers," recalls Kaz. "It was Gretzky's move that put aluminum in the marketplace."

"But marketing the new aluminum stick needed help," remembers Gretzky's agent, Mike Barnett. When the original sticks came out in a dull brown colour, Barnett took the aluminum stick to a friend who polished it to a glistening silver sheen. "When Wayne used this bright new silver stick in his first game," recalls Barnett, "Harry Neale called it 'Gretzky's Silver Excalibur' on TV." And a stick legend was born.

Gretzky used the Easton stick until his final years in the NHL, and while a number of his peers – including Bossy, Brendan Shanahan, and Phil Housley – also adopted the aluminum stick, the product was destined to lose market share to other technological innovations in succeeding generations of players. Whether it was the better feel of wood or the control afforded by graphite, aluminum was doomed. "I think I'm one of the last players in the league using aluminum," said Detroit's Shanahan in 2001, in his fourteenth NHL season. "I always tell Easton, if you're going to discontinue, give me the opportunity to buy about a thousand sticks to get me through the rest of my career."

The next contender in the technology sweepstakes was the Titan/Turbo, the brainchild of Karhu. Bossy was the guinea pig for the Turbo in the 1985 season. It used the principles of foam injection developed by the ski industry to create a lighter, stiffer shaft; in the Turbo, a fibreglass shaft was injected with these same foams to provide strength and stability. Then a wood or a laminated wood and plastic blade was inserted in the base of the shaft.

"This dramatic innovation in hockey-stick design is yet another leap forward in the quest for excellence in the field of hockey equipment technology," trumpeted the Titan PR campaign. "It feels like an explosion!" Bossy was quoted in the same ad. Today, the Hall of Fame winger, now a broadcaster and restaurateur, still raves about the first models of the red stick he used. "I have to say that when it first came out, it was the greatest stick I ever played with. It was light, and I could play and practise for a month with the same stick. It was the stick I scored my 500th goal with. Titan sticks were known for being heavy, and to be honest, I was glad for something lighter in my hands. But it was inconsistent. I'd get only four or five out of the dozen that wouldn't break near the heel."

Bossy's enthusiasm eventually flagged. "I never thought I was fussy, but I guess people would tell you that I was," he laughs. "I liked a stiff stick, and I was very particular about the curve. But I'd get a batch that were great and a bunch that were junk. They just couldn't make them the way I wanted them. My last year, I used a stick painted red at the factory. I don't think it was the Turbo, but the manufacturer wanted it to look like the Turbo." The foam-injected technology died soon afterwards, except in goalie sticks. Turbo's technology became – and remains – the norm for NHL goaltenders, but not for skaters.

Graphite, or plumbago, is a hexagonally crystallized allotropic form of carbon. With its metallic lustre and greasy feel, it's found in everything from lead pencils to nuclear reactors. A weave of its fibres can produce extremely strong, flexible materials. When sports manufacturers began using graphite in tennis rackets in the 1970s, they found it delivered an ideal blend of power, control, and easy care, even for the weekend warrior. Despite a daunting price tag, graphite rackets supplanted aluminum models during the 1980s. In golf, too, graphite was revolutionizing tastes and prices. Graphite clubs offered lightness, consistency (they retain their stiffness within five degrees for the life of the club), and fatigue resistance – the ability to spring back to shape after impact.

In hockey, the long-term prospects for graphite sticks
would depend on several factors. First, graphite technology
had to be inexpensive enough to persuade consumers to give
the new sticks a try. Initial costs of up to $75 for a com-
posite shaft and $20 for a blade made – and still make – this
type of stick a steep investment for the hockey parent or
recreational player. But the successful introduction of
graphite in the other sports was proving that people would
pay handsomely for a technology that really worked and
was really durable. This was no small issue in hockey, where
price is considered the major factor affecting buyer deci-
sions at the store.

Second, the manufacturers of graphite sticks also needed
pro endorsements to reach a retail market ever more reliant
on NHL exposure. As the Gretzky-Easton marriage had
shown, that issue could be addressed by getting the right
young players – Paul Kariya, for one – to use your stick.
Within a decade, Easton's graphite stick had ten per cent of
the total market.

Third, the graphite or composite stick also had to be
demonstrably more reliable than wood or aluminum, a prob-
lematic challenge for manufacturers. The first wave of
graphite sticks created a mild sensation when they came to
market in the early 1990s, when Gretzky's move from
Edmonton to the Los Angeles Kings expanded the frontiers
of North American hockey. Again, Easton was among the
pioneers. But reliability problems proved irritating; even a
bang against the bumper of a car could crack the shaft.
During the introductory phase of composite sticks, in fact,
breakage became a safety issue as flying shards from the

sticks caused injuries to players and some fans. People shied away from graphite, but manufacturers gradually refined the composites, incorporating graphite, fibreglass, and Kevlar, and after a lull in the late 1990s, sales boomed again.

By 2000, Easton was producing the Synergy, the first viable, synthetic one-piece stick in the NHL. "There's other companies trying to make them, but nobody seems to get the feel like Easton," says Red Wings equipment manager Paul Boyer. "The Synergy makes a big difference," agrees playoff ace Claude Lemieux, who switched to the Synergy in 2001. "When they first came out with the blade and the shaft, I felt they lost a lot of torque in the bottom part of the stick. But now they've perfected it to a point where I'm getting used to it. With a wood stick, the puck doesn't bounce off the blade as much. But you get a lot more snap out of the Synergy than you would from a wood stick."

The 1988 Canadian federal election was dominated by the issue of free trade with the United States. Having earlier said that the free-trade issue had been decided by Reciprocity in 1911, Brian Mulroney, the Conservative prime minister, shifted positions as easily as Gordie Howe switched hands to shoot the puck. Mulroney sought a mandate to conclude the North American Free Trade Agreement, a pact with the United States that would reduce tariffs and encourage the flow of goods between the two nations. His opponents, led by Liberal leader John Turner and NDP leader Ed Broadbent, argued that the deal would surrender Canadian sovereignty and weaken domestic industry.

The debate about how much commerce with America is enough is as old as Canada itself. As a nation founded partly in reaction to the American Revolution and U.S. expansionism, Canada has always guarded its resources from "Yankee domination." After Wilfrid Laurier signed the Reciprocity deal in 1911, he was driven from office by a furious electorate and the captains of a captive economy.

No industry was more central to Canadian interests than the forest industry and its subsidiaries – including the business of making hockey sticks. The debate that gripped the country in 1988 pitted those who treasured Canada's past and its culture against those who felt the future in a globalized world lay in closer ties with the Americans. Quebec sought an open U.S. market for its hydro power; Ontario quaked at the threat to its manufacturing base. In the end, of course, Mulroney's Tories defeated Turner's Liberals and won the go-ahead for NAFTA. The impact of that monumental deal is still being assessed, but its effect on the tiny world of stick making is clear. A new order has arisen. Canada still dominates the wood-based stick industry, but wood is steadily yielding ground to composite sticks, and the United States – with mega-corporations producing space-age components for almost every sport – now dominates the production of composite sticks.

That doesn't mean Sher-Wood is ready to quit. While its market share has been cut, the company used the 1990s to get its house in order. Leo Drolet retired in 1990, having taken a small francophone business to world status in his forty-one years at the helm. Drolet had been perfect for his times, and after his departure the stories about him became mythical. Leo was never a fan of coloured sticks, and one day he was vexed to see a large order of yellow- and pink-coloured sticks ready to ship.

"Where are your damn pink sticks going?" he growled at his son Michel.

Told they were going to a Swiss client, Leo grabbed the phone to call Switzerland. "Who wants these sticks?" he demanded of his distributor. Told that a large client liked them and would order more, Leo barked, "You'd better be sure. Because if these sticks leave this factory and you don't like them any more, you're going to eat them."

Under the leadership of Leo's son Denis, the original owners repurchased the company from Adirondack Industries. Sher-Wood accounted for about twenty per cent of global stick sales in 1997, down from the glory days of the mid-1980s, when they had a thirty-five per cent market share, but still enough to make them a major player. That market share is all the more impressive when you consider that Sher-Wood doesn't produce its own aluminum or composite sticks (they do, however, cooperate with the Swiss firm Bush, which produces composite sticks).

Not that Sher-Wood or its competitors have ignored the advances in their industry. In 1993, Sher-Wood invested $1 million in automation and new technologies for its plant. The company has subsequently adapted many of the materials from the composites – such as Kevlar and carbon-graphite – into its blades and shafts. In 2000, CCM carried the Groove Lite shaft that features hollowed-out channels combined with a blade wrapped in Kevlar, and the 2295, a wood shaft with graphite in the core. Louisville, meanwhile, introduced a shaft in which a layer of graphite is covered by Kevlar and then by a wood exterior.

Manufacturers of wood-based sticks such as Sher-Wood still hold one trump card over composites: price. While the shift to composite sticks in the NHL has been noteworthy, wooden sticks are still the more popular choice for minor and recreational players. At $10 to $40 a stick, they handily outsell aluminum and composite sticks, which range from $30 to $350.

According to industry wisdom, a stick's price is the number one factor governing consumer purchasing. "If the price is beyond the consumers' individual price point, he will not buy the stick no matter how good it feels," says a 1997 company circular from Bauer sticks. But price is only one of the considerations. According to Bauer, a consumer decides to make a purchase as follows:

Step 1 – Graphics and Cosmetics (ranks sixth in importance)
"Strong graphics are very important if you want the consumers to take a closer look at your stick, although they become far less important in the actual purchase decision."

George Kaz remembers how important graphics can be. In the mid-'80s, when KOHO/Titan/Canadien saw its market share fall off, the company looked at coloured sticks as a marketing device. "And I mean colour," laughs Kaz. "So we brought out a teal green stick with silver on it – which was never done – and we put that on the rack of a Mercedes. We came out with black sticks with pink in them and blue sticks with orange. And we gave them names like the KOHO

Revolution. It was a marketing plan that said, 'Look, basically a stick is a stick is a stick. This is just a packaged goods
deal. So we're going to revolutionize the business by changing the labels.' Some of the initial reactions were 'You guys
are nuts, you can't do that shit, you're going to get blown out
of the water.' Within a year, we had gained all the numbers
we'd lost. Our market share started to fire up again."

Step 2 – Brand Loyalty (ranks third in importance)
"Many players buy Sher-Wood for no other reason than because
it was the first stick that their parents bought for them."

Steve Davies describes a stick purchase as "a self-serve
impulse buy." But impressions are enduring. "It's a very
personal thing. There's a tremendous loyalty to the last purchase. If you had success with the Hespeler 5500 with a particular heel curve and it was the Gary Roberts model, you
go back looking for that same Gary Roberts model."

Step 3 – Performance Characteristics (ranks second in importance)
"All other things being equal, this is the reason for choosing a particular stick."

Howie Meeker was taught how to choose a good stick years
ago, when he was with the Leafs, by CCM rep George
Parsons. "I'd pick up a dozen sticks between the thumb and
forefinger and bounce them. You'd find three or four that
were better than the others, then bounce them again to get
a couple that had the right flex. It's still the only way to pick
out a stick on the retail market today. They put a dozen

sticks in there and eight of them are dogs. Too big, too heavy in the handle – no adults can flex the damn thing."

Step 4 – Price (ranks first in importance)
"This is perhaps the most important of the buying criteria."

"Look at the dominance of composite shafts in the NHL," points out Steve Davies, "and then look at composites as a portion of retail sales in hockey. The trickle-down effect is not there. And it's because it's price sensitive."

Step 5 – NHL endorsees (ranks fifth in importance)

Consumers tend to deny the value of marquee appeal, yet testing proves its efficacy. Sher-Wood learned the value of player endorsements early on, with Ken Dryden. "When we saw him in the net," recalls Georges Guilbault, "with his hands folded over the end of his stick and the name Sher-Wood in full view, that was a real publicity coup."

Step 6 – Retailer Sales Influence (ranks fourth in importance)
"When it comes down to the moment of actual purchase decision, they are your best marketing department."

With the cost of equipment rising rapidly, consumers now look for more knowledgeable staff and proper fitting. For this reason, the small hockey retailer – with trained staff who know customers personally – still holds nearly a third of the market for sticks and other hockey equipment, despite being outgunned by department-store chains and "big box" sports retailers. Stick companies encourage the health of these shops through seminars and courses, if only to minimize returns and short-circuit angry customers. They understand that most consumers must trust a merchant to lay out up to $250 for a stick.

Despite the marketing strategies and packaging gimmicks, the sourcing and grading of new wood is crucial to every successful Canadian stick manufacturer – as it was a century ago to the Mi'kmaq. In recent years, decimalized machines have become the norm. "They don't even do this with the wood you use in your house," says CCM's Marc Vosteen, pointing out the new machines for grading wood on his shop floor in Drummondville. "Your roof could come down because you don't have this stuff. Here, our wood could hold up a house. Even better, we could tell a contractor that in ten years, this piece of wood will be better than that piece. We're at that point now. All this happened with the demand for lighter, more consistent, stiffer sticks."

Like the introduction of composites, this improvement in wood has brought increased lifespans and prices for sticks. It has also brought unused capacity to the factories. "Most of the hockey-stick manufacturing facilities were built when products were made to break," says Davies. "They didn't design them to break, of course, but they didn't have fibreglass reinforcement in the shaft. Nowadays, everything lasts so much longer that these facilities have production that doesn't run at 100 per cent."

Excess capacity has allowed "cyber" stick manufacturers – companies with no physical home – to arise. "Nike makes lots of sporting products," Davies points out. "Eight billion units a year or something. They don't own any factories. What they have are proprietary designs for equipment. They have other people build it for them. That's what we have now, too. I don't need someone to go out and grade a 100-flex shaft for me in a stack of wood. I say, 'I want a nineteen-ply wood shaft,' and there are a limited number of places you can buy it. The characteristics from any of the sources are very acceptable. You're taking a shaft with a spec, a heel joint with a spec, and marrying it to a blade with a spec and a tolerance and a thickness. Then you apply a graphic to it. I hate to say it, but it's that simple."

Today, shafts can be sourced from anonymous factories in Coboconk, Red Lake, or Cornwall, Ontario, or from plants in the Eastern Townships of Quebec, or from plants in the United States. Blades are designed, built, and added at another factory. In some cases, graphics and cosmetics are applied at a third location. As a result, the mills, drying kilns, and processing yards are being eliminated at most factories. The yard at Sher-Wood's plant by the St. Francis River is littered with dead and dying machinery. "A hockey factory used to be sandpaper – little conveyor belts with sandpaper shaving the sticks," says Marc Vosteen. "Now there's all these machines controlling the sandpaper, testing the weight. In the last ten years, the stick has gone from A to Z. We can do anything imaginable to a hockey curve. In Lafleur's time, they curved sticks by hand – using hot water, judging by eye. I'd go out back and tell the boys how to do it. Now, machines do everything."

Ironically, the most prominent manufacturer of "cyber-product" carries one of the most venerable hockey names:

Hespeler. The acquisition of the name came about by chance, says Steve Davies, who resurrected Hespeler in the late 1980s. The Toronto-born Davies had been a math major who'd played college hockey at Lake Superior State in Michigan for four years and then pro hockey in Germany for another season before returning to Canada. When a friend, Eric Niskanen, suggested jobbing sticks to retail outlets, Davies was unsure. "As a math major, I guess I had ideas of doing something better than schlepping sticks out of a garage." Having nothing else on his plate, however, Davies gave the stick business a whirl. With a bunch of new stick manufacturers coming into the market at the same time, their timing was perfect. He and Niskanen became the largest distributor of sticks in the country with their company, International Stick.

Like most hockey aficionados their age, Davies and Niskanen revered the great old brands they'd grown up with, such as Northland and Hespeler. The Hespeler name had disappeared when Cooper purchased the company in 1972. "Around 1987, we were talking over a couple of beers and saying, 'What ever happened to Hespeler sticks?' We said, 'Why don't we put forth a trademark application and see what happens?' So we put in the application and, lo and behold, we get a letter from the government saying the name's ours. That was when they [Canstar] were breaking up the assets of Charan Sports, which owned Cooper sticks. In the midst of all this restructuring, the trademark application sort of slid through unnoticed."

International Stick eventually got into the business of modifying some of the sticks it handled for specific customers.

That included special-product designations, such as the Sher-Wood 5030 HMP model, made for them by the Sherbrooke manufacturer. Davies's experience had shown that you no longer needed a home factory to be in the stick business. He and Niskanen decided to revive the newly acquired Hespeler name on a range of sticks for which they held the design specifications.

First, though, they had to fend off the legal challenge of Canstar, now aware they'd lost control of the Hespeler name. After a spirited battle, Canstar relented and Davies emerged triumphant with the name – and not much else. The factory on Sheffield Street still belonged to Canstar. They had to find factories to manufacture their products – and fast. Having dealt with the major players for a decade, Davies knew that in the brave new world of component manufacturing, factories operated at less than top capacity. There was always going to be enough slack in the schedule for a competitor to step in and make use of the facility. At the Hespeler plant itself, and later at other plants in Ontario and Quebec, Davies purchased time to produce his Hespeler sticks for the NHL and the broader market. (Later, pursuing his goal of component manufacturing, he extended the Hespeler brand name to include skates and other equipment.)

Solving the manufacturing riddle was easy for Davies. It took a brush of luck from a friend in the NHL to get him the marketing exposure he needed. In 1989, Davies had sold his interest in International Stick back to Niskanen and set out to make Hespeler a household name again. He needed NHL endorsement, but how to get suspicious pros to try his unproven stick? He got his chance during hockey's most visible annual spectacle: the Stanley Cup final.

Colin Patterson of the Calgary Flames had known Steve and Eric "since childhood," says Patterson, now a businessman in Calgary. "I'd run into them at a friend's wedding in the summer of 1988. They told me they were going to revive the Hespeler name and I said, 'When you get some, send them to me.' But nothing happened that fall, all that season. Then, on the eve of Game Six in the 1989 Stanley Cup final, these sticks arrive in Montreal. I was walking around, showing them to everybody. They were red and they were ugly, but what was I going to do? I'd already told everyone I was going to use them."

Davies picks up the story: "So at the morning skate, here comes Patter with his Hespeler, and the guys start giggling – 'Where'd you get that, at a gas station?' I go back to the hotel and flip on the TV and I couldn't believe it – Patter was using the stick. And he scored on Patrick Roy in the first period, and the Flames won the game and the Cup."

"It was my first shot in the first period," recalls Patterson. "Chris Chelios was trying to clear, but I intercepted it. I put a little snapshot on net that beat Roy low on the stick side. I raised my stick up and I don't know why, but I kissed it. I'm on the ice, hugging the guys, saying, 'Who needs one of these sticks?' That picture was on the front of the *Journal de Montréal*, the *Toronto Star* . . . all over the place, with the stick straight up in the air. I had a buddy who saw it in a paper in Hong Kong. You could see 'Hespeler' clear as a bell in the photo." And it was a start.

The next year, 1990, the NHL instituted steep licensing fees, charging manufacturers of branded equipment worn by players during league games. The fee scared off Davies until Patterson's celebrated Flames teammate, Doug Gilmour, adopted the Hespeler stick. "We were in training camp in Prague," recalls Patterson. "I'd been playing well with the stick. So Gilmour takes one of my sticks. Because of the licensing fee, he rubs out 'Hespeler' and puts 'Canadian Tire' on the shaft as a joke. Then he goes out for the warm-up and shoots the lights out in practice. That was it. Soon we had lots of guys on the Flames using it – Gary Roberts, Joe Nieuwendyk, eight guys. I went to Buffalo in a trade and pretty soon we had five guys there using it." When Gilmour himself was traded to Toronto, in 1992, he took the reborn Hespeler with him. "It was a series of good experiences and exposure that worked out well for us," says Davies. "That was the rebirth of the brand."

In 1997, Davies sold Hespeler to First Team Sports, an American firm based in Minnesota, while staying on as president. That meant he had a new partner – Wayne Gretzky, who owned a piece of First Team Sports and thus now owned twenty-five per cent of the name made famous just north of his own birthplace of Brantford, Ontario. Gretzky himself used a Hespeler in his last year in the NHL. Hespeler sticks – a brand pulled out of the archives – are now made at four locations in Quebec and Ontario.

In an era that has seen the demise of Eaton's and the rise of Wal-Mart Canada, the near-extinction of small, independent bookstores and the creation of big-box Chapters and Indigos, the disappearance of community newspapers and hardware stores and corner groceries, Steve Davies longs for the days when hockey sticks said something distinctly

Canadian – the days when they emanated directly from the towns and villages of the country's heartland. He's done nicely by Hespeler, but he's not entirely sure that Hespeler and other towns like it have done as well by globalization.

Steve Davies could be referring to any number of things when he laments, "This business is becoming impersonal. Anyone could bring a product to market, because there's lots of outsourcing opportunities. Throw some money at a high-profile player, give him an equity position in your brand, then out-source whatever you need. There's not a lot of people hanging their hats on the growth of companies through proprietary technology. The world's become a branded nightmare. It's a branded nightmare out there."

CHAPTER 5

THE FIRST BANANA

It's almost an illegal weapon.

Former NHL goalie Chico Resch

Like many inventors, Stan Mikita stumbled on his discovery. "Stash" – Mikita was born Stanislas Gvoth in Czechoslovakia in 1940, and adopted the name of the uncle who helped raise him in Canada – was a tough, gifted centre for the Black Hawks (the team's name at the time) from 1958 to 1980, when back problems ended his prolific career. His four scoring titles, two Hart Trophies, six First-Team All-Star berths, and 1,467 career points won him a place in the Hall of Fame. After earning a reputation for truculence, Mikita turned pacifist. From seasons of 150 minutes in penalties, he ended up spending only 12 or 14 minutes a year in the box. In a team game, he was an individualist.

One day in the mid-1960s, the Black Hawks were winding

down toward the end of practice at the cavernous old Chicago Stadium. "My stick cracked," recalls Mikita, whose scarred face bears testimony to the art of suturing. "On the blade, the backhand side. It wasn't a clean break. It was still in one piece on the forehand. The crack itself almost turned it into – what do they call that thing? A boomerang. And I thought, 'Oh shit, I've got to get a new stick.' "

A teammate was watching from the other end of the ice. "He tried to break it," remembers Bobby Hull, whose golden locks and Adonis frame contrasted with Mikita's wiry intensity. "That's what he usually did. I'd say, 'Don't do that, I've got a hundred kids who'd like that stick.' But he'd break it and throw it over the boards toward the organ. This time it wouldn't break, so he jammed it into the door of our bench. It was so live and willowy it still wouldn't break. When it came out of the door it looked like this –" Hull's massive hands form a C-shape. "Stan pounded on the glass. That was the signal for the trainer to come up the twenty-two steps from the dressing room to see who it was, then go back down to get a new stick." In the old Chicago Stadium, the dressing rooms were below the ice surface and a round trip for the Hawks trainer, Nick Garen, took several minutes.

"Out of anger," says Mikita, now a businessman in Chicago, "I slapped a puck against the boards, hoping to break the stick. Well, it didn't break, but I noticed when the shot hit the boards the sound was a little different. I also noticed the puck took off a little different. It felt like I really caught the whole puck, so I slapped another one and another. Then I took a wrist shot. Then it finally broke." A curious Hull skated over to ask what he was doing. "When I tried

Stan Mikita is generally thought of as the inventor of the
curved blade—this is his model—though other players,
notably Andy Bathgate, beg to differ

to break my stick, I put a hook in it," Mikita told him. "Can
I ever snap the puck!"

When Mikita got back to the dressing room, "I started
bending sticks till they broke. Someone said, 'They bend
easier if you wet them.' So I ran a couple under hot water.
To keep it in a bent position, I got a chair and put it under
the handle and put the blade under the door. It stayed that
way overnight and the next day it was dry. So I taped it up
and worked on it, then went out and started shooting, won-
dering what might happen. Well, the first slapshot I took
acted like a knuckler in baseball. It dropped and veered. The

next shot did all sorts of things. In the meantime, Bobby's watching me. So he started bending his, too."

Mikita refined his innovation, opening the face like a golf club to get a little lift and moving the curve closer to the toe of the blade so as not to affect his backhand. When Mikita was ready to try it in a game, Hull decided he'd try his left-handed curve as well. Chicago coach Billy Reay was not impressed. "You guys can't use them," he said. "I mean, shit, you can't control them."

Hull's first game with the banana blade underscored Reay's concerns. "The first shot he took, he shot it over the glass," chuckles Mikita. "Well, he damn near killed some people." In another game, Hull hit Ranger goalie Gump Worsley in the head. "You could hear the thwack all over the building," remembers Mikita. "Fortunately, the flat part of the puck hit him and he wasn't badly hurt." An unfazed Worsley, asked if he feared the curved blade, replied, "I think the people in the first rows behind me are in more danger than I am."

Chicago's highly strung goalie Glenn Hall – who had the unenviable task of seeing the two gunners in more than 100 practices a year – played it safe. "He'd hug the post, and out of sixteen shots, he'd give you an effort on maybe four," says Mikita. "We'd say, 'C'mon, Glenn, you gotta try.' Then we started hitting him, and he'd come chasing after us. We didn't want to hurt him, of course, but he took it real seriously."

Hall's woes increased in 1964 when Bobby's brother Dennis showed up on the Hawks with a slapshot that many said was even harder than that of his famous brother, if less accurate. "Bobby could shoot the puck through a car wash and not get it wet" went the line. "Dennis would do the same, if only he could hit the car wash."

It took Mikita a while to master his innovation. "I was never going to shoot it hard enough, because of my strength versus Bobby's strength. I mean, he was 200 pounds. His arms were like my legs. I asked Bobby, 'Besides your strength, where do you get the speed and the heaviness on your shot?' He said, 'Geez, I don't know, I take some ice before I hit the puck. . . .'

"So when nobody was around, I experimented with hitting the puck right on the edge first, hitting it with a quarter inch of ice, a half inch, then an inch of ice before I actually hit the puck. And I tried to bend as much of the handle as possible. I say tried to – when you're moving fast and especially when some son of a bitch is trying to knock your ass off, you can't be that precise. I came to the idea that it's like a golf shot, technique has a lot to do with it. But the bigger guys have a better chance of hitting it farther."

Gradually, Hull and Mikita mastered the diabolical properties of their curved blades. In 1965–66, Hull became the first man to top 50 goals in a season, breaking Maurice Richard's record with a 54-goal blitz. In 1968–69, he fired 58 bullets past bewildered goalies. Mikita, meanwhile, won the Art Ross Trophy as the NHL's top scorer in 1964, '65, '67, and '68 – by which time, needless to say, many other players around the NHL had adopted the curved blade.

Every major innovation in the stick has sparked a revolution in the style of play, and Mikita's was no exception. The original one-piece Mic-Mac was strong and durable, but short and unyielding for shooting. It was ideal in a game in which goals were usually scored in close to the net and low to the ice. Before the advent of the centre red line in 1943, coaches emphasized a pressing attack, forechecking in the offensive zone, and knocking home defensive mistakes. As a result, the "hot zone" for goals extended no farther than twenty feet from the net. Hard shots from the blue line were unheard of. (Anyone who's played shinny on a public rink would recognize the style.)

By the 1920s, goaltenders had come to dominate this style of game. NHL teams, constricted by rules that prevented passing across blue lines and limited by the one-piece stick, averaged only 1.4 goals a game. Montreal's George Hainsworth racked up a goals-against average of 0.98 in 1928–29. The men running the NHL were not happy with this scoring rigor mortis, and neither were the fans. In 1929, the league allowed forward passing within the neutral and defensive zones. It proved an instant success – one most experts attributed to the rule change. But the changes wouldn't have had such an effect without the simultaneous introduction of longer, livelier, two-piece ash sticks, which facilitated more accurate passing. The two-piece stick, pioneered by Hespeler and St. Mary's in Ontario, also made possible shots that were harder, higher, and more accurate, forcing lightly protected goalies to cover more of the net. Strong players such as the Leafs' Charlie Conacher, "The Big Train," began launching wrist shots at up to 50 mph. The souped-up sticks pushed the arc of scoring back thirty feet or more from the net. NHL scoring almost doubled.

The offensive liberalization of the game was accelerated in 1943 with the introduction of the centre red line, which encouraged head-manning the puck out of the defensive zone. An expanded scoring zone and unlimited passing meant teams could no longer afford to concentrate on the area directly in front of the net. Better skaters and bigger defenders were needed to keep hard shooters like Bill Cook and Nels Stewart on the periphery of the scoring zones and to prevent teams from passing the puck behind the defence. Head-manning – Montreal's fire-wagon hockey – was devised to emphasize break-out strategies and speed in the counter-attack, and the strategy remained virtually unchanged for twenty years.

In the era of the two-piece ash-handled stick (from before World War II until the first NHL expansion in 1967), NHL scoring hovered just below six goals a game. And there it stayed. Max Bentley's league-leading 61 points in 1945–46 (in fifty games) would still have placed him among the top five scorers two decades later. In many seasons in the 1960s, Bentley's prorated output would have won him the Art Ross Trophy as the league's top point getter. The Original Six era may be the hockey connoisseur's favourite for its intense rivalries and star power; it certainly wasn't distinguished by innovations in tactics or equipment.

The mid-1960s proved a time of change and ferment on many levels in Canada, from the emergence of the independence movement in Quebec to the introduction of a new flag. On the streets, Canadians witnessed the more expressive individualism of the counter-culture; in the nation's arenas, they witnessed a more offensively charged style of hockey. The twin innovations of the curved blade and the slap shot conspired to shatter scoring records. The popularization of the slapper by players such as Boom-Boom Geoffrion (ironically, his nickname came from the sound his shot made when it missed the net and hit the boards) and the emergence of the curved blade had boosted average scoring to 8.3 goals a game by the 1980s.

Other, more subtle, changes to the stick also tipped the balance in favour of shooters. Three-piece sticks introduced by Sher-Wood in the 1950s gave blades greater flex and ability to stand strain. Stronger athletes such as Geoffrion, Hull, and Frank Mahovlich could really lean into their CCM or Northland models, catching just the right amount of ice behind the puck for maximum whip. Teammates recall the shaft of Geoffrion's stick bending like a willow branch as he cranked his big shot.

How hard did Hull or Mahovlich fire the puck? Dozens of players today – including Hull's son Brett of the Dallas Stars – shoot as hard as they did. But to opponents in flimsy equipment, Bobby Hull's bombs were a fearsome revelation. "A couple of times he broke my shin pad and the skin underneath," says former Detroit rearguard Doug Barkley. "We learned to get up close to him, because it didn't hurt as much if you were in close." Barkley grins. "I didn't have that much trouble with Bobby. He came down the other side. But my partner, Marcel Pronovost, he had real trouble."

The curved blade allowed a shooter to cradle the puck in the microseconds of contact between blade and rubber, increasing velocity. Tinkering with the loft – the blade's variance from the upright – accentuated the dips and turns that made a ninety-mile-an-hour slapper so dangerous. Even smaller players such as Mikita, who weighed only 160 pounds, and Montreal's Bobby Rousseau, who weighed about 150, could, with a curved blade, load up like the big boys.

With the marriage of slapshot and curved blade, NHL scoring levels began their steep rise and manufacturers took a crash course in the production of the banana blades. Kids across Canada antagonized their coaches by showing up for games with sticks better suited to sixty-foot cannon shots than feathery backhand passes. And why not? The scoring zone now stretched out to the blue line and beyond. Fired by the likes of the Hulls, Mahovlich, Vic Hadfield, Rod Gilbert, and Yvan Cournoyer, shots sailed past startled goalies from unheard-of places. Offensive marks weren't simply bettered, they were shattered. Within seven years of Mikita's fateful Black Hawks practice, the single-season goal-scoring record soared to 76 (Esposito); the points record rose from 96 in 1959 to 152 in 1970–71 (again Esposito). Even defensemen were getting in on the act; Orr tallied an unthinkable 46 goals and 135 points in 1974–45.

As if they needed the help, shooters were soon aided by dramatically lighter fibreglass sticks that made possible even harder shots; by the mid-1980s, defenceman Al MacInnis, then of Calgary, was clocking 100-mph slapshots on radar guns. This power surge outstripped anything goalies or their flimsy equipment could come up with – they were simply overpowered by improved technology in the hands of bigger, stronger athletes. Three decades of target practice, in short, and all of it due to Stan Mikita.

Or was it?

Leaning against the boards at the old Maple Leaf Gardens
in the uniform of the NHL All-Star Legends, silver-haired
Andy Bathgate, nearing seventy, looks as if he could still
skate a couple of shifts in the NHL. The 1959 winner of the
Hart Trophy, he scored 349 career goals in an era when
goals were at a premium. For the woeful Rangers, he potted
40, 35, 30, and 29 goals in separate seasons, on a team that
usually missed the playoffs.

Bathgate says he used a curved blade as early as the 1940s.
"Back in Winnipeg, where I grew up, my brother Frank and
I used to curve our sticks. We'd get them wet and give them
a nice bend. It helped us to raise the puck. I used them all
the time, even when I got to junior in Guelph. When I got
to the Rangers, my coach, Alf Pike, would go around stepping on the blades to break them. 'You can't use those in a
game,' he'd say. When he was gone and Phil Watson came
in, I started curving them a little more."

Bathgate thinks Mikita might have got his idea for the
curve from him. "Chicago was in to play us one Saturday
afternoon at Madison Square Garden – it was one of those
CBS TV games, I think – and Stan had run out of sticks. I
guess their trainer went to our trainer to see if he could
borrow sticks for the game – we were both right-handed
shots. I had some I was using that had a little curve in them
and so our trainer lent them to Stan. I think he just took it
from there."

Mikita is less than receptive to the Bathgate version. "I
told Andy to his face that he's – well, let's say I talked to him
about it. I might have borrowed some sticks, but I sure don't
remember any curve. No, mine started with the breakage of

the stick." Bobby Hull suggests a compromise: "Andy was before me. He broke in full-time in 1954 and my first year was '57. I remember his stick always had a little hook in it. But Stan was the one who really pioneered."

Bert Olmstead, meanwhile, says he was curving sticks in his youth in Alberta in the 1930s. "Oh, we used to curve them all the time. That's how we lifted the puck. They were so whippy that when we got them wet, it was easy to curve the blade." Olmstead says he and other NHL players put slight curves in their blades when the vigilant eyes of their bosses were trained elsewhere.

The debate over the origins of the curve is like the argument about which Europeans first reached North America. Archaeological evidence proves that the Vikings and the Basques reached our shores hundreds of years before Columbus, but Columbus has always had the best PR. Bathgate may have led the way to the new frontier, but Mikita has always had the best spin. Besides, Mikita's version of the banana blade is the one that sparked the mass movement away from the straight blade. Indeed, within a decade of his accidental invention, the straight blade was virtually dead in the NHL level. (So were more than a few goalies.)

If Mikita was unsure exactly how he turned his stick into Excalibur, Stephen Murphy can clear up the confusion. Murphy's day job is with Bauer/Nike Hockey in Montreal, where he's director of product research for helmets and gloves. But he's also Captain Slapshot. He's studied the shot in minute detail; his Ph.D. thesis at the University of

Waterloo was entitled "Three-Dimensional Dynamic Analysis of the Ice Hockey Stick During the Stationary Slap Shot." As a catchy title it may need work, but Murphy knows whereof he speaks.

In an office overlooking the old Blue Bonnets Race Track in Montreal, dressed in golf shirt and slacks on a hot July afternoon, Murphy seems a far cry from the mad hockey scientist. A native of Elliot Lake, Ontario, he was a rink rat who channelled his love of the game into the quest for a better stick. "There's no other Ph.D. doing what I do in hockey," he says from behind a desk heavy with research papers, printouts, and hockey tape. Murphy played on a couple of northern Ontario championship teams in the OHA and later played university hockey at Waterloo. He's a specialist in biomechanics, having done his master's degree at Ottawa University before adding the Ph.D. at Waterloo. In between, he started working for the forerunners of his current employer, Canstar. They encouraged him in the hopes of reaping the benefit of his research. Within months of this meeting, Murphy's findings will be incorporated into a new product: the Tri-Flex stick.

Murphy believes the usual design process for sticks puts the theoretical ahead of the intuitive. "People have been doing static tests – weigh the stick, do a three-point scan to see how much the stick deforms, come up with a flex number – but is that what actually happens in a slapshot? That's what we're investigating, different design approaches. What do players need to take a better shot?"

Murphy broke down video to 2,000 frames per second to study the minute changes that occur during shots, using players from pee-wee right up to varsity. From these break-downs he developed computer simulations to study what happens to the stick. He loads his computer to show a visitor a three-dimensional hockey hologram winding up, powering the cyber-stick, and then following through. "This enabled us to isolate events at the blade level, the shaft level, and the resulting velocity of the puck," he says, rotating the image from a side view to an overhead perspective.

Murphy attached strain gauges at key points on the shaft to measure the deformation of the material in the stick during a slapshot. "It's like a rubber band. If I take a really inflexible band and stretch it and let it go, it won't snap back a lot because it's too stiff. But if I have the right stiffness and the right stretch – wow! It really snaps.

"A player hits the ice about forty-five or fifty centimetres behind the puck, contacting the ice first. The first thirty centimetres are just bringing the blade tangentially to the ice – you're just skimming, you haven't lost any velocity yet, you're getting the biofeedback of being comfortable with where you are. It's happening quickly, in ten milliseconds. You're just ramping up, the load is two kilograms – five pounds – not a lot of weight down vertically yet.

"When you get close to the puck – about fifteen or twenty centimetres – you start leaning into the shaft, loading up the blade. Then you hit the puck with the blade. The puck is made of rubber, and the new blades are made from material that actually 'noodles' around the puck – the impact deforms the blade. That can make the puck move ahead of the blade, which isn't good because you're chasing it. But most of the time you're loading the puck onto the blade, and unloading it on the follow-through. The puck is on the blade 3.5 milliseconds, about seventy times longer than a golf ball is on the face of a club. By comparison, a golf ball stays on the club face about .5 milliseconds. Golf is pure impact."

Al MacInnis of St. Louis, the 1999 Norris Trophy winner, has long had the hardest shot in the NHL. Even nearing forty years old, he still fires lasers. MacInnis credits his big slapper to a boyhood of booming a thousand or more pucks a day against the barn of the family home in Inverness, Nova Scotia. Murphy says all that hard work is evident. "Where you contact the puck on the blade is very important, and MacInnis hits the puck in almost exactly the same spot every time. He's very consistent."

But the secret of MacInnis's shot goes beyond simple accuracy. "He has one of the longest sticks in the NHL," observes Murphy. "That means he can generate a higher blade velocity with a longer arc. To use a fancy term, there's a lot of strain energy involved. That means there's the right combination of flexible rigidity and the proper deformation of the materials in the stick. The longer the stick, the more strain energy you've got."

MacInnis's heel curve (a curve located closer to the heel of the blade than to the toe) is another key to his hard shot. Murphy props a blade on his desk to illustrate. "If I'm impacting the puck, it starts right here at the heel. When I deflect the blade back like this" – he shows a puck striking the blade at the heel – "it goes through there and then forward, because it's very stiff here. That's why a heel curve must be stiff. If I have a uniform curve in the middle, the puck tends to roll off to the end of the blade. You lose accuracy."

Blade science has come a long way since the days when Mikita and Hull used hot water and a door frame. One innovation has been to rocker – or curve – the underside of the blade. "If you look at the original curve that Hull had, it didn't have a rocker. When a rockered blade comes through, more of the blade contacts the surface on the ice. With Hull's flat, curved blade, it was supported at both ends, but you had a gap in the middle that was off the ice."

Murphy says MacInnis embodies another key to launching a puck 100 mph or more. "There's evidence to suggest that a young player doesn't know how to use his legs, how to bend his knees. He's more upright, giving it a sweeping blow without putting his weight behind the shot. But look at MacInnis – he's bent at the waist, transferring his weight from the back leg to the front leg, which allows him to generate energy, to deform the stick because he's loading it up while it's on the ice."

What about the wrist shot, for almost a century the weapon of choice for the game's great players? What has allowed players from Howie Morenz to Pavel Bure to score so many goals without a windup? "It's obviously a much slower motion," says Murphy. "You have to wrap your wrists over" – he grabs a stick and rotates his hands on the shaft – "so that they work against each other. I mean, if you watch some of the goals Bure scores, he's got his hands wrapped way around like this, so he can go up top with the shot.

"Looking at the wrist shot from a design perspective, that's where the curve in the blade is more important in your ability to 'load' the shaft. A stick designed for a slapshot – a stiff stick – isn't necessarily good for a wrist shot."

When a visitor asks why one stick can feel so different from another, Murphy grabs several models from a rack on the wall. "There's a lot you can do to change the feel of a stick. There's a way to make a stick feel lighter without changing its weight. You can make the blade lighter and put that weight in the middle of the shaft. You haven't changed the weight, but because you moved the centre of gravity up the shaft it feels lighter. It's analogous to a trip to the beer store. How is it easiest to carry a case of beer? It's easier to carry it at your belly button, the centre of your body, because that's where your centre of gravity is. You don't get rocked forward or back.

"One thing that's happened, we've made our composite shafts very light, but we haven't made the blades lighter. So the centre of gravity has moved down the stick. If you lighten the blade, you move the centre of gravity up the stick to where it's easier to manipulate. You can't move the centre too high, of course, or the stick will feel top-heavy."

After decades of shafts of uniform stiffness, Murphy has helped develop a stick technology explained by a bow and arrow analogy. "You look at a bow and both the tips can flex, but the centre is very stiff. In the Tri-Flex, we're looking at three zones. You have the flex in the top hand of the stick and flex down toward the blade. But in the middle, where the lower hand is, we're making that very stiff. We think this design is closer to the natural processes of the slapshot than taking a mechanical or manufacturing approach."

The idea is to achieve torsional stability in a lightweight construction. Murphy compares a Porsche and a big station wagon. The Porsche is light, with a tight suspension to allow for fast cornering. The station wagon is bigger and stronger, but because of its sloppier suspension, if it takes the same corner at the same speed, it rolls over.

Murphy is part of a new generation seeking to quantify hockey's unholy arts, to translate words such as "feel" and "balance" into numbers. Want to know how stiff a stick is? In the old days, when Bobby Hull went to McNabb's Sporting Goods in Belleville, he'd lean on each stick, trying to find one whose wood fibres offered just the right combination of stiffness and flex. "My dad would say, 'Go in and pick one out,'" Hull recalls. "I'd grab one and lean on it. My dad would say, 'Oh Robert, just grab any one.' I'd say, 'No, there's one in here that's got my name on it, and I'll know it when I feel it.' Finally, I'd hit the one that was balanced, had the right snap to it, the right weight. That's the way I picked them out."

When Hull was a kid, manufacturers gave sticks suggestive names like Tuff-Bilt and Roc-Hard. Nowadays, they use what they call a flex rating – that is, stiffness expressed in kilonewtons at five centimetres of deflection. A 15.0 is a medium flex; a 21.0 is labelled XX-Stiff, fit only for the likes of the mighty Eric Lindros, who adds a couple of blade wraps for extra stiffness just as a precaution. They'll also produce a lie (the angle of the blade to the shaft) of anywhere from four to seven. A number five lie is 45 degrees; each increment up or down corresponds to 1.5 degrees. Wayne Gretzky used an almost-unheard-of number four for much of his career, because his hunched-over style dictated a flat lie. By contrast, MacInnis employs a number seven, which suits his upright style.

In days past, almost every player would shave, file, rasp, and blow-torch his stick's handle to suit his particular grip. When Conn Smythe mandated twenty-two-ounce sticks for the Maple Leafs back in the '40s, Howie Meeker carved as much as five ounces off his stick to make it light enough to handle. More recently, tough guy Tim Hunter of Calgary was renowned for the hours of meticulous preparation he spent on his sticks under the stands of the Saddledome – this from a plugger who ended up with just 62 goals in his seventeen-year career.

Today, thanks to malleable materials such as graphite and aluminum, manufacturers offer ergonomic handles – concave, convex, square, oval. You can order virtually any shape to suit your grip, even on composite models. A finicky player might have a concave grip for his top (or power) hand and a convex grip for his lower (control) hand. Along the way, this evolution has produced a new vocabulary fit for a hockey Einstein: anisotropic, extrusion, isotropic, pultrusion, chem-fused, creel, fibre adhesion, filament winding, horizontal laminate, polymer composites, resin transfer moulding. Still, it all comes down to how the stick feels in a player's hands.

There are tales of almost preternatural sensitivity among players who agonize over their sticks. Sher-Wood executives were astonished when former NHL centre Ken Linseman told them he could tell whether the factory worker had cut the wood for his blade on the inside or the outside of the pencil mark. "I didn't believe it, not a bit," says Michel Drolet. "I did tests several times and Kenny was almost always right. He just had to hold the stick on the ground to tell if it conformed exactly to the pattern."

Claude Larose, a journeyman forward with Montreal in the 1960s and '70s, was forever changing sticks to get a more comfortable feel. One season, he changed his pattern four times before Christmas. After much fussing, he finally settled on a pattern he liked. His game picked up, and he told Michel Drolet how pleased he was with the new model. Drolet took him aside. "Claude, I'm your friend, so I want to let you in on something. The last model we worked on corresponds exactly to the first model we developed for you."

A nonplussed Larose replied, "Well, the problem must have been my skates."

Ironically, one of the most indiscriminate stick users was the best offensive player the game has seen. Grateful stick representatives called Gretzky the ultimate "zero-maintenance" guy. Gretzky tore apart NHL scoring records in his early days using a white Titan TPM 2020, which has been described as "a log," "a rock," and "a railway tie." "Did you ever see one of Gretz's sticks?" asks an NHL equipment man. "There's no one today who would use it."

That Titan may have been heavy and unresponsive, but in the hands of the master it was a magic wand. In Edmonton in 1981–82, he set the marks of 92 goals and 212 points in a season. In the late 1980s, he was lured to Easton's aluminum stick, another model about which stick experts are less than enthusiastic – particularly in the stick's early days. "Aluminum was very limited," says Stephen Murphy. "You couldn't get it as lightweight as you wanted. It was cold in your hands, it didn't have good dampening properties. It just wasn't the solution." Thus handicapped, Gretzky counted "only" 163 points in 1990–91.

In his final season, 1998–99, when Gretzky became an owner, and thus a proponent, of Hespeler sticks, an all-ash replica of the old Green Flash was created to honour the origins of the stick in western Ontario. "We made one up with a six-inch graphic on it that looked like the old Green Flash of thirty or forty years ago," recalls Steve Davies, the president of Hespeler. "Well, somehow it got into the Rangers dressing room and he went out and played with it. He played the first period with basically a thirty-year-old hockey stick and had no problem with it. Anybody else would have gone for a skate and said, 'What are you, crazy? You can't play with this.' There are guys who have such soft hands it doesn't matter what they're using."

Meeker, too, marvels at what the best players can do – even with the wrong stick. "Rick MacLeish played all his life with a stick six inches longer than anybody else's," recalls Meeker. "But he made it work, scored all kinds of goals for Philadelphia [349 career goals]. Reggie Leach, too, had a stick that was way too long, but he made it work." (Meeker believes, by the way, that long sticks are the bane of minor hockey. "Our kids have no puck-handling skills and with ninety per cent of them it's the length of the stick. I saw the Canadian women's team the other day and one of their players had the same problem, losing the puck under the stick when she tried to handle it. It's the mothers of this country who are running hockey and controlling the length of the sticks. They're saying, 'If my kid wants a long stick, they're gonna have a long stick. Don't you dare cut it.'")

The vagaries of stick preference are always a source of amusement and speculation when NHL players get together. Claude Lemieux, the peripatetic winger who has accumulated four Stanley Cup rings and a legion of enemies for his abrasive style, is one of the connoisseurs of sticks, a noted stickler for detail. "Go see Peppy, he's the best," says author Roy MacGregor. Lemieux has earned a reputation as a "closer" for teams looking to win a Cup. After helping Montreal to its 1986 championship, he joined New Jersey for the Devils' 1995 win, moved to Colorado to help the Avalanche win the next year, then returned to Jersey and helped the team salt away the 2000 Cup. Whichever stick he uses, it must be doing something right.

The search for Lemieux finds him working for Gretzky in the Phoenix Coyotes' dressing room. With his stocky build, deep-set eyes, and leathery face, Lemieux could pass for the bad guy in a French *cinéma noir* classic. At the mention of sticks, however, a boyish grin crosses his face.

"My stick is very basic," he says, even as teammates snicker in the background at his perfectionist ways. "It's like you'd find in a retail store. Nothing special. I think they've perfected the Synergy to a point where I'm just about getting used to it. With a wood stick, the puck doesn't bounce off the blade as much. But in return, you get a lot more snap out of the Synergy than a wood stick. The new generation are going with those sticks. Within ten years, you'll have ninety-nine per cent of the players using graphite sticks. It's tough to compete with graphite. It's too bad for the guys who make wood sticks.

Adam Oates sports one of the NHL's oddest-looking sticks, a
stubby-bladed model that helps him perform as one of the
league's most gifted playmakers

"It's fun to see other sticks, how much every one is different. With graphite, not everyone gets their own pattern like they do with wood sticks. So it's easy for the stick companies to keep them supplied. Adam Oates . . . now his stick is definitely unusual. Have you seen it? He's got like half a blade. You have to see it. Kovalev in Pittsburgh, he's got a big banana blade, hardly any blade on the ice. Everybody says, the more blade on the ice, the better the shot, but he's got a rocker with no blade. Jagr, too, has a big toe curve. But you should see Oates's stick, if you haven't already."

Sure enough, the blade of Oates's Sher-Wood model looks like it survived an encounter with a meat cleaver. About three-quarters of the way to the toe, the blade is truncated vertically. It appears as if the manufacturer simply knocked off early for lunch and forgot to finish the stick. Oates talked about his stick one day after practice in the Washington Capitals' dressing room.

"Most of the guys laugh at it," says the smooth centre who's made a living feeding snipers from Cam Neely to Brett Hull to Peter Bondra. "They try to use it, then throw it away and say it's ridiculous. They say, 'What are you doing with a kid's stick?' "

How did Oates arrive at such an unusual model? "It's funny, I used to have a rather long blade. I was in Boston and got a shipment of sticks that were all cracked . . . broken close to the toe. I didn't want to waste them so I cut them and used them for practice. Cut them off square at the end and they felt okay. They worked perfectly along the boards. The balance in the stick shifted higher up the shaft. I started using them in games, and I did okay. A while later I tried to go back to the old blade but it wasn't the same. Since then I've lengthened the shaft a little, and Brett Hull showed me how to rocker the blade." It's hard to argue with success: Oates, one of the most skilled playmakers in the league, has more than 1,200 points in his career.

When it comes to extremes, however, no one has topped Kent Douglas. Sitting on a sofa at the Royal York Hotel in Toronto prior to the 2000 All-Star Game, Douglas hardly looks the type to have used a gargantuan stick. He's a compact 5-foot-10, and his playing weight ranged from 180 to something over 200 pounds. Using grit and what looked as savage as raw lumber, he picked up three Stanley Cup rings with the Maple Leafs. In pre-Bobby Orr days, he notched a respectable 33 NHL goals in eight seasons – not bad for a stay-at-home defenceman. But that hardly sums up his career. In the years before and after the NHL expansion of 1967, Douglas did the Hank Snow tour of North America: Kitchener, Winnipeg, Vancouver, Springfield, Toronto, Rochester (three times), Tulsa, Oakland, Detroit, Baltimore (twice), Long Island, and Toledo. Have club, will travel.

"You know," he recalls, "the guys from Sher-Wood or CCM would come in the room and look for some great big guy. They figured nobody else was going to use a stick like that. Well, I did, and I liked it. And I've got pretty small hands. I don't have long fingers either." Despite this, the 1963 NHL Rookie of the Year used a stick almost twice as thick and heavy as most of his teammates' sticks. "It started when I was playing junior in Kitchener in 1955. I could go over to where the stick plant was [in nearby Hespeler] to get the kind of lumber I wanted. I wanted a heavy, big stick – it's easier to hold onto. The puck would hit it and stay right there. I'd see a lot of guys' sticks and the puck would bounce right off, you know? I'd pick them up to see if they were heavy enough. If the shaft or handle bent when you leaned on it, I didn't want it. I wanted something with very, very little movement in it. The ones that weren't balanced I didn't want, either."

How did he manage to lug this tree around the ice, trying to keep up with the likes of Henri Richard and Yvan Cournoyer? "My first job in the summer was working in the mines near my hometown of Cobalt. I worked in the mines when I was fifteen. You were supposed to be sixteen. First job I had, I was the guy with the sledgehammer. I guess going from swinging a sledge to picking up that big stick wasn't really a big transition."

Douglas used different sticks in different situations. "I used to have three sticks – one for the power play, one for regular play, and one for penalty killing. They got heavier as you went along. For penalty killing, I'd skate to our bench – the benches were real close together – and say, 'Give me a log.' Of course, they could hear you on the other bench."

Considering Douglas amassed 631 penalty minutes in 428 games, his request for heavy lumber could have meant only one thing to his opponents. Stan Mikita remembers Douglas's stick – and not fondly. "It was the biggest handle I'd ever seen, a two-by-four. He took a swipe at me once in Toronto and hit me over the head. I wasn't wearing a helmet. The blood came out like the fountain of youth. I took a good forty stitches on the outside. I don't know how many they put on the inside."

Douglas also liked a steep lie. At a time when the average lie was a five, Douglas used a nine, the shaft seemingly at right angles to the blade. This eccentricity set him apart, and in the pre-union days of hockey, being too individualistic could spell trouble for a journeyman player. When Douglas was sent to the Springfield Indians and their notorious owner Eddie Shore, he wondered what was in store. "I'd come in from Kitchener and he met me at the train," he recalls. "We talked about sticks and stuff like that. He says, 'What lie do you use?' I say, 'You probably don't have any – I use a nine.' Turns out he believed no one should use anything less than a six, so my nine didn't bother him at all. Shore's idea, especially for defencemen, was if you handle the puck here, at your feet, whoever was checking you had to get in close. And if they were that close, they shouldn't get the puck away from you. There was method to his madness."

Douglas's Springfield teammates who liked a shallow lie secretly had number five lie stamped as a six. Eventually, in 1967, the Springfield players rebelled against the autocratic owner, persuading him to sell the team to Jack Kent Cooke, who had just started the Los Angeles Kings. Shore may have been gone, but he wasn't forgotten by Kent Douglas. "My feeling," he says, waving across the lobby at former teammate Billy Harris, "has always been that the old man knew more about hockey than anyone before or since."

CHAPTER 6

MERCHANTS IN THE TEMPLE OF HOCKEY

A salesman is got to dream, boy. It comes with the territory.

Arthur Miller, *Death of a Salesman*, 1949

A bright morning in October, game day for the Detroit Red Wings at the Calgary Saddledome. In the concrete cavern beneath the stands, Vince Maillet looks like a hockey version of a street vendor. He's spread his wares on the concrete floor around him, the latest products from the Montreal-based Hockey Company, which now includes CCM, KOHO, Titan, Canadien, and Jofa. Early in the season is the best time to shop the newest goodies to the lucrative pro market, and there are sticks without blades, blades without sticks, pants turned inside out, gloves with fingers cut open, everything for the contemporary player. As the twenty-eight-year-old Maillet patiently waits for his chance to launch into his pitch, Andreas Johansson and Wade Belak peruse his wares, their muscular legs bulging beneath track shorts.

Across from Maillet is Doug MacInnes, his rival from Sher-Wood, with the latest from the Sherbrooke-based manufacturer. (Ironically, it was MacInnes's move to Sher-Wood that opened the position at The Hockey Company for Maillet.) While Maillet uses Calgary as his base of operations, MacInnes covers the west from his home office in Winnipeg. Beside MacInnes lie more sticks of varying lengths and composition, with blades of all colours and shapes.

Down the hall stands Gary Linquist in his spiffy Easton jacket. He's here with the newest from the Easton labs in Van Nuys, California. The one-piece Synergy stick, introduced in spring 2000, is still a hot seller for the company, which began by making arrows for archers in the United States. Dave Campbell of Bauer/Nike is due tomorrow. These are the merchants in the temple of hockey, and no one is about to toss them out any time soon. The sound of cash is religion in Gary Bettman's "branded" NHL.

"This is the 2295," Maillet tells a passerby, cradling the sleek new stick. "That's the wood shaft with graphite in it. The 1052 CCM is the one that's hollowed out – it's called the Groove Light, with a layer of birch and two layers of fibreglass. They hollowed it out, all the way down." Sure enough, looked at from the top, the shaft is honeycombed, as if termites had worked their mischief on the birch. It's also incredibly light. "When we tested in Finland last year, it had a wood blade and we found that the shaft would outlast the blade. So we went with the graphite carbon blade instead."

Today's challenge for Maillet is the 6-foot-5 defenceman Belak (now a Maple Leaf). The hulking young native of Saskatoon uses a sixty-three-inch shaft, the longest permitted in the NHL, which he cuts back slightly for better handling. The blade on his CCM is similarly large. "His blade is the maximum length and width you can get," Maillet explains. "It's not even a hockey stick any more. It's a paddle. I mean, his stick is taller than me. I'm 5-foot-10, and his sticks are taller than me."

Indeed, Belak on skates is almost seven feet tall and three feet across the shoulders. He's like a skating billboard. No wonder he needs a veritable telephone pole. Even he would admit that his stick hasn't been minutely calibrated for scoring; like Kent Douglas's old model, it's made for moving forwards and clearing pucks. "I find that the big blade is best for stopping pucks as they come around the boards," explains the boyish Belak. "You don't get it jumping over top of your stick like you might with a smaller blade. I started using it in junior and I've gotten used to it this way."

"You can't be too pushy with the NHL guys," confides Maillet, watching the massive Belak flex and bend the new products. "You talk to them, show them the new things. You may see them two or three times and then all of a sudden, they go 'You know, I'm going to try this.' Some guys it takes time. Others, they'll try it right away, like Denis Gauthier [of the Flames]. He used wood for years and years. Last year, he didn't want to try a composite at all. This summer he flexes it and says he wants to give it a shot."

Maillet is a kind of hockey Willy Loman, but for this salesman there is wonder and excitement in keeping the best

MERCHANTS IN THE TEMPLE

players in the world equipped. "It's not like an insurance salesman, where the consumer doesn't really want to be dealing with insurance. This is different. They want to do this. They enjoy it. When you're fitting them, they're happy. It's the best industry in the world as far as I'm concerned."

As the pro rep in western Canada for The Hockey Company, Maillet services the three NHL clubs in the west, plus the junior Western Hockey League and the Manitoba Moose of the International Hockey League. Like the rest of his brethren, he loads his vehicle – in his case, a GM van – with CD player, tape deck, cell phone, and a ton of gear and makes a circuit of western communities that breathe hockey history: Medicine Hat, Swift Current, Kamloops, Prince George, Brandon, Price Albert . . .

"I did 82,000 kilometres last year," he says. "That doesn't include nine flights to Vancouver and four to Winnipeg. It's definitely not the type of job where you want to have three kids and a wife. They'd never see you. I've got the whole nine yards in that van to keep me on the road, keep me awake. At one in the morning, when you've still got two more hours of driving, you learn to pull over for a coffee."

Like most people who service the hockey market, Maillet grew up playing and loving the game. That affection has been tested by his share of late-night phone calls, when disembodied voices tell you, "The sticks aren't here – they were supposed to be here today." It keeps a rep on his toes. "You deal with the likes of Mark Messier and Phil Housley, you're dealing with the big boys, and they're pretty finicky. You don't want to screw up. You want to get it right the first time."

Still, after working in sporting goods retail in Saskatoon for ten years, he's thrilled to be dealing with NHL players. "My first day was here in Calgary, and Denis [Gauthier] was the first guy I talked to. He helped me out, made me feel comfortable, introduced me to some of the guys. I'll respect him for the rest of my life for doing that. Messier, it's been a while since I saw him, but he was very good to me, too. Every time I was in the room, he'd remember my name, shake my hand, say hi. He didn't wear one piece of my equipment and he still acknowledged me. That was nice of him, and that's what you need."

You need patience, too. Some players are fanatical about their sticks. Brett Hull is the NHL version of "Tool Time," travelling with hacksaws, sandpaper, files, rasps, blowtorches, hair dryers, aerosol paint, and several colours of tape. He prepares three sticks a game, often customizing them to the style of play he expects that night. "If you're going to be in a close-checking game, you might want to do things that help you get the shot away faster – making the stick lighter. In a wide-open game you might want a heavier stick. Not that we play many wide-open games any more."

A few players take the care of their sticks to another level – Jeremy Roenick, for example. "I kiss them and rub them and, you know, show them lots of love," he says in the Phoenix Coyotes' dressing room after practice one day. No one is allowed near his Easton aluminum models. "If a guy grabs my stick, or if another guy's stick touches it, I'll go take a new one that's nice and fresh and virginized. I get vocal about it. I'll give a quick little scream and tell them to stay away. I'm very particular about who touches my stick, how it's curved, the weight. I'm constantly on the phone to

Easton, letting them know if the blades are too thick, if they're too heavy, if the shafts are too whippy. That's my bread-and-butter, what makes me score goals. If you're not comfortable with your stick or skates, you struggle."

As a teenager in Massachusetts, Roenick went to practices at Boston Garden to collect broken sticks for his basement. He modelled his current pattern on the one used by Bruins great Rick Middleton. "He had the coolest stick. It had a nice little upshoot, and I kind of curved mine after his. The upshoots, you can make them as big as you want and they're legal, instead of having a plain middle curve. I stay away from fines for illegal sticks." Provided no one touches his stick inadvertently, Roenick uses about one stick a game.

Petr Klima, the former Red Wing, Oiler, and Lightning, kept a stick only until he scored. Then he broke it, in the belief that each stick had only one goal in it. Gretzky, in his prime, went through six sticks a game, some 700 a year, though he rarely broke one. In part it was superstition, in part the voracious demand for souvenirs.

Players have been known to name their sticks (Rick Vaive called his twenty-five-ounce Titan "Big Bertha") and even talk to them, especially when they're slumping. Phil Esposito, while GM of Tampa Bay, took this a step further, talking to the stick of his sputtering gunner Mikael Renberg. A Tampa player was startled to see Esposito in his office giving a pep talk to Renberg's lumber. "You can do it," crooned the man who himself never had trouble finding the net (717 goals in 18 seasons). "Tonight's the night, baby, you can do it." (The encouragement obviously failed. Renberg was dealt to the Flyers not long afterwards, and Esposito was eventually fired as GM.)

A hundred variables go into a player's choice of stick. And players are particular when they find something that works. When it stops working – when a goal drought hits, or the puck rolls off the stick too often – players can abandon a pattern faster than you can say "polymer composite." Is the stick to blame? Hardly, but if you're Andreas Dackell, say, and the scoring gods have abandoned you, you look at anyone else's model you can lay your hands on.

Dackell had only two goals for Ottawa in the first half of the 1999–2000 season after scoring 15 the year before. Shots were missing the net or getting buried in the goalie's pads. Some said he missed his centre, Alexei Yashin, who was holding out for a new deal. Others said the 15 goals had been a fluke. Dackell didn't know what to think. After a brutal stretch of twenty-six games without a goal, he went looking for salvation.

He found it in a bundle of Joe Sakic Easton sticks that arrived at the Corel Centre. Dackell grabbed one, flexed it, tested it for balance, then had the Easton rep convert Sakic's left-handed models to right-handed for him. His season turned around; he scored eight goals in the second half of the season and his overall game picked up. Did the stick make him a better player? Or was it just the odds kicking in for him after a long slump? Like most players, Dackell wouldn't want an answer to those questions. A player's bond with his stick is one of hockey's mysterious imponderables. Call it superstition. Call it whatever you like. Just don't mess with success.

Clarke Wilm of Calgary is one of hockey's cowbirds, adopting whatever pattern works for a teammate before flying off to another model. Exasperated reps have given up on trying to stock a consistent pattern for him. Pros who flit from one design to another can be costly for manufacturers, who must stock expensive casts costing up to $5,000 and designs for players. "We had a couple of players who would have a ton of their sticks sitting on our racks," recalls George Kaz, "and it got to the point where we didn't want to work with these guys any more because of the costs. They're going, 'I dunno, it's off like a nano something, . . .'" But with the salaries paid to top players nowadays, nothing about the craft is left to chance.

Including a little constructive discipline. When Bruce Gardiner of Ottawa was still looking for his first NHL goal after fourteen games with the Senators, he decided he'd been too kind to his sticks. At the urging of teammate Tom Chorske, Gardiner exiled his sticks to the toilet stall in the dressing room. Sure enough, he scored twice in his next game with the chastened stick. Now, whenever a Senator has a scoring slump, his stick ends up doing solitary in the john.

In the cramped visitor's equipment room at the Saddledome, Paul Boyer is ministering to the Red Wing troops. He's unpacked his portable skate sharpener, and many of the forty-odd bags and trunks used to carry the Red Wings' gear are arrayed on the floor around him. Against the wall stands a forest of wood, aluminum, and composite sticks –

the Red Wings' arsenal. At the moment, defenceman Aaron Ward is rummaging through one of the equipment bags.

"What are you after?" asks Boyer, looking up from his skate sharpener.

Ward holds up the blade on his Bauer stick. The heel is frayed and the black tape is ripping away to reveal a nest of battered wood fibres.

"How'd you do that?" a visitor asks.

"See this?" smiles Ward, a player not renowned for his puck-handling skills. He bangs his hands on the table. "Rock solid," he jokes. "These hands are used for dumping it hard, icing it, or lobbing it."

"In the other bag," says Boyer, his boyish face breaking into an insouciant grin. Ward goes into the bag to find a new blade for his stick. "He blows out a blade a day," mutters Boyer as he returns to sharpening skates. "You want to know about me?" he asks incredulously above the low whine of the machine. "I was born and raised in the Soo. Played minor hockey there. Went to Lake Superior State, was equipment manager there for five years. One year with the New Jersey Devils. I've been seven years with the Red Wings. Won two Stanley Cups while I've been here. Love the job."

As equipment manager, the youthful Boyer is the gate-keeper, the conduit between the approximately twenty-five stick companies and the Detroit players they hope will use their product. Boyer does all the equipment purchasing for the Wings, and a good working relationship with him is a must if you want to do business. "You've gotta keep in touch with the equipment manager, that's key," says a stick rep. "With all the stuff coming in the door, it's more work for him. The more work you make for him, the worse it's going to be for you – trust me."

"I tell all the stick reps that I don't sell the equipment, that's their job," says Boyer. "I just make sure that if they sell it to them, we have the stock. Every rep meets with me before they leave my building so I know who they've spoken to, what's going on. They'll say, 'I've got this new shaft – I'd like to give it to this player.' And I'll say okay, or maybe I'll shy them away because that player is endorsing a certain company."

In hockey's tribal culture, a star can steer teammates toward a company he likes. In Detroit, captain Steve Yzerman is king, and he's an Easton man. After using Louisville for many of his most productive seasons (he had 228 goals from 1987–88 to 1990–91), Yzerman switched to the Easton composite. A cursory examination of the stick rack this day reveals a number of teammates who've followed his lead. "Players do seem to follow the leader," says Boyer, placing Slava Kozlov's one-piece Easton Synergy back in the rack. "They seem to like what other guys are using. There are a lot of right-handed shots on this team, and of course Stevie's right-handed. Everybody tried one of his, and there was a time when [Darren] McCarty was using it and [Mathieu] Dandenault was using it and [Martin] Lapointe was using it. I can give them my two cents' worth if they ask, but there are good salesman out there who'll service a guy. Once they get a guy using their stuff, they're good at it."

Boyer nods in the direction of the three stick reps just around the corner, hoping to interest the passing players in the latest product. "It's a jungle out there for equipment right now. Especially at the pro level, because the exposure drives your retail sales."

What's the most important factor in fitting a pro player to a stick? "The lie," says Boyer. "They want to make sure they have enough blade on the ice, so the puck doesn't jump over their stick. When the sticks come in, I always try to make sure they're happy with the lie. You can always change the curve. The players know their stick, they know what they want, where the curves and upshoots should be. If they tell me it's wrong, I believe them, because their sticks are their life."

The conversation turns to the curve on Kozlov's one-piece composite stick. Flat on the ice, Kozlov's blade appears to lean forward; halfway up the blade, it seems to change its mind and tip over backward. "That's probably the most dramatic curve on our team," says Boyer. "That's what Alex Delvecchio's stick looked like. I have it at home. It looks like a helicopter blade. It's bent one way at the top so he could stand back and roof the puck. It's actually pointed forward at the bottom. If I showed it to you, you'd laugh.

"And Phil Esposito – what a boomerang on that. I don't know how he controlled the puck, but he scored a ton of goals."

Detroit wingers Lapointe and Dandenault poke their heads in. "Where's the soccer ball?" says Lapointe. Boyer fishes a soccer ball – great for training – out of a net bag on the floor. "Hey," he says to the visitor, "you want a good story about patterns, go ask Shanny. Don't tell him I sent you."

Brendan Shanahan is getting out of his practice uniform in the dressing room nearby. The tough, prolific, veteran winger is one of the more approachable players in the game.

"I'm supposed to ask you about your blade pattern," says the visitor.

"Did Wally [Boyer's nickname] send you?" laughs Shanahan. "It was when I was with St. Louis. I don't remember exactly, but I think I'd run out of blades before they could ship more – the dreaded snowstorm in Montreal – so I went out and I used Garth Butcher's blade. I probably had a good game, so when my next batch came in, I sent them back and said, 'Scratch out "Butcher" and put my name on it.' If I ran out or broke too many after that, I'd just go to Butchie directly."

Shanahan going to Garth Butcher for a scoring remedy is like the governor of the Bank of Canada going to a credit union teller for fiscal policy. In fourteen NHL seasons, Butcher amassed a grand total of 48 goals. Through fourteen NHL campaigns, Shanahan has 452. Yet Shanahan uses Butcher's blade pattern. Go figure.

"Brett Hull's a connoisseur of sticks," adds Shanahan, stripping off the shoulder pads he's worn since minor hockey. "I got a lot of grief from him. He'd got me to change the knob on my stick from something the size of a puck to what it is now. When he saw I was using Butchie's stick, he just shook his head and said, 'You scored fifty goals, I'm not going to argue.'

"So we had a competition, because Kelly Chase [also not noted for his scoring touch] used Brett's blade pattern. Who would score more goals – Garth Butcher and me together, or Brett and Kelly Chase? Usually Butchie would outscore Chase," Shanahan chuckles, "but Hullie would always outdo me."

By staying with an aluminum shaft, Brenda Shanahan finds
himself one of a dying breed—a holdout against the growing
acceptance of composite sticks

One of four brothers of an Irish immigrant clan in west Toronto, Brendan and his brothers were adept at both hockey and lacrosse (his brother Brian played pro lacrosse). After a brilliant junior career in London, Shanahan became the second choice overall in the 1987 NHL draft, going to New Jersey. Stops in St. Louis and Hartford preceded his arrival in Detroit and his two Stanley Cups as a Red Wing. He's a multimillionaire these days, of course, but in his youth his father found it a challenge to keep his brood supplied with sticks.

"He'd go out to the Canadian Tire on the Queensway and find some special at the start of the year and buy a dozen sticks. This is like the early '70s. We each got three sticks to do us for the year. I think he had a deal with someone, because he'd get them between the back door and the garbage bin. You'd try slapshots with them and they'd break because they were all dried out. We had three righties and one lefty in the family and we were all angry at Brian, the lefty. Because of Brian my father bought straight sticks. That was the deal. He'd say, 'That's twelve sticks for all of you, and this will do you through to next season.' They were all straight because he wouldn't break the dozen.

"I hated the kids on the street that bought these white plastic inserts. You'd grind them on the sidewalk so they were a toothpick and would raise the ball for them. I started with a really bad wooden stick and guys used to make fun of it. It was a real wimpy stick, and I had a wimpy shot. I stayed with the wood, though, and started really working on my shot. Obviously I got bigger and stronger and I was always trying to find a wooden stick that wouldn't give. I hit a lot of ice with my shot – if I was a golfer I'd have big divots – so it got to the point where my stick was just a log in my hands.

"It was in New Jersey, probably my third year in the NHL. The wooden ones got to the point where I said, 'I need it stronger, they're giving too much.' The wooden stick was great for shooting, but by the end of the first period my forearms were aching from holding it. Then they came out with aluminum. I still go through about two shafts a game. Go look at the warpage on my sticks in the rack. And if you're playing in a beer league in a cold rink, it'll promote tendinitis in the wrist and elbows. You get that twang when you hit the puck sometimes in a cold rink. I don't take too many one-timers in that case, because you feel it right up to your shoulder.

"But if you talk to Easton, you'll find the only time I complain is when they change something. You know, everybody's switching now to graphite. I tried it for a month, and I hated it. I don't know whether it's mental or not. That just shows you the sorry state of hockey – I consider myself a purist because I use aluminum!"

From the door, coach Dave Lewis gives Shanahan a sign: time for the bus to the hotel for the pre-game meal. "Sorry, I have to go. We've got a lunch meeting at one. . . ."

As the visitor leaves the dressing room, Boyer, by the door, is sorting through a bag of extra shafts. "I'm fortunate in Detroit," he says. "We haven't made that many personnel moves, haven't had a lot of guys in and out. Over time you get to know what they want and what they need." With that, Boyer returns to the business of sharpening skates. "The door opens every day, and the puck drops every night," he says, as the whine of the sharpener again fills the room.

CHAPTER 7

STICK IN TRADE

One could do worse than be a swinger of birches.

Robert Frost, "Birches," 1916

The puck dropped every night for the Original Six teams, too, but that was a world far removed from attentive equipment managers and solicitous stick reps. The sticks of yore were expected to last, and cost-conscious managers made sure they did. "We had about six sticks at a time," recalls Andy Bathgate, who broke into the NHL full-time with the Rangers in 1954. "If we broke a stick or needed new ones, we had to go to our equipment manager. He'd give us a voucher for three sticks. Then we'd go to Gerry Cosby's Sporting Goods around the corner from the old Madison Square Garden, hand them the coupon, and they'd give us our new Northlands. You couldn't get extras or anything like that."

Things were no better in the benign dictatorship known as Maple Leaf Gardens. A few players had custom sticks. Syl Apps, the stylish captain of the fine Toronto teams of the postwar period, had his sticks made for him by Sher-Wood, but such players were few and far between.

"Oh, it was terrible," laughs Howie Meeker, who played with the Leafs from 1946 to 1954. "Tommy Naylor, he looked after the sticks in his skate-sharpening room – a dark, dingy place. If you had six sticks in the rack, you were lucky. They were hard to come by. They were all CCMs, too. George Parsons, the ex-Maple Leaf who lost an eye, he worked for CCM as the go-between. He'd see that we had a supply of sticks. I don't really remember breaking sticks, it wasn't a problem in our day. But if you broke them, you had to go see Tommy. He was great, he'd say, 'Take as many as you want, just don't get me into trouble.' At home, I kept about six sticks – three in the dressing room and three in the rack in Tommy's office. We only took three sticks when we went on a road trip. I mean, that'd sometimes be for four games – three sticks.

"One time, both [Bill] Barilko and [Garth] Boesch broke their sticks in the same game – same shift, in fact, going down to block shots. And the next day Smythe comes in, looks at all the sticks and says, 'They're too light.' And that's where the rule was made that all our sticks had to weight twenty-one or twenty-two ounces."

Not much had changed in Leafland by the time Carl Brewer arrived in 1958, five years after Meeker's departure. "It was like pulling teeth to get new sticks," Brewer recalls. "The guys today, they get any number of sticks, whereas the sticks were husbanded very closely by the training staff in my day. I would basically use a new stick every game, so I would go through at least seventy a season, probably more. I was always having to get new sticks from Tommy Naylor."

Doug Barkley remembers that sticks weren't a big issue on his Red Wings of the 1960s. "They used to last a long time," he remembers. "Our captain, Alex Delvecchio, could make a stick last two weeks. The trainer would just tape them up again, and he'd play with them. Every week, a guy from a local sporting goods store would bring over a few new ones. You'd try them out, but it wasn't like today, where guys go through a dozen sticks sometimes just to get one."

In the conservative climate after the war, there was little value in a player's lending his name to a stick. Even Gordie Howe's endorsement didn't sell sticks, as Jack Lacey discovered. Lacey, the owner of Wally sticks, recalls, "I had Gordie tied up pretty tight for ten years. But when we went to sell a stick with his name on it, we ran into resistance. 'We're not going to pay you anything extra for Gordie's name. Who's he think he is?' See, this was before big names got real popular." When Gordie's wife, Colleen, asked to be released from the deal so they could sign with Eaton's, Lacey didn't shed any tears. "We paid him so much per stick sold. We didn't sell too many."

The advent of the curved blade and increased competition from new suppliers in Canada and Europe helped open the floodgates. By the end of the 1960s, NHL players were being openly courted to use something other than a CCM or a Northland. And in the heated competition, they were soon paid considerable sums to use sticks in games.

Howe's endorsement deal with Eaton's was the first major one featuring an NHL star. His name on TruLine equipment and sticks represented the perfect marriage between legendary player and famous national retailer. While it didn't make Howe rich, the deal prefigured the endorsement explosion to come – one powered by television. Once restricted to Saturday nights, hockey games became more frequently available on TV. The proliferation of hockey imagery in people's living rooms allowed regional companies to take their pitch across the country.

By the time stick companies began courting players in earnest, around 1970, their goal seemed to be to buy up as many NHL players as they could. Whether you got their loyalty through cash or contra deals, volume was the goal. The thinking was that the more players you had in a high-profile media market such as Toronto, Montreal, or New York, the better. The more often a fan saw the logo, the deeper the brand penetration. At one point in the 1980s, Sher-Wood boasted that fifty per cent of all NHL players and ninety per cent of all American Hockey League players used their sticks. That was thought to be a lot of productive publicity.

Other stick producers made it a point of pride that they never paid players. "The boss came one day and he said, 'Look, we're not paying anybody to use our stick,'" remembers Walter Anderson, who worked with Jack Lacey at Wally and then at Louisville. "If they want our sticks, we'll make them for them, but we're not paying them. We can sell all the sticks we make without having to pay somebody."

Other companies, such as Sher-Wood, avoided direct payments by employing players as part of an "advisory staff" that received exclusive service and consideration in exchange for the use of their names. "Guy Lafleur never asked for a single cent from Sher-Wood for using our sticks," says marketing man Georges Guilbault. "Not a cent! But he demanded service in spades, let me tell you."

By the end of the 1970s, though, most companies did pay fees, the size dependent on a player's production and his visibility in major markets. A couple of superstars, Gretzky and Mike Bossy, each got close to $50,000 a year for endorsing Titan. In the meantime, Canadian retailers — Loblaw's, Labatt's, Roots — were discovering the power of branding, and hockey marketers began to notice that money spent on middle-rank players didn't affect market share. Only superstars provided real return on investment. George Kaz, who came from a background in retail marketing, says the experience of Titan/KOHO/Canadien with their marquee players — Bossy, Gretzky, and Lemieux — convinced them to reduce their stable. Faced with three separate brands to market and not many differences among them, president Doug Barber decided a new strategy was needed. "What came up through focus groups was that Titan had appeal to the kid market," recalls Kaz. "Wayne was on the cusp of becoming great, a year away from those 180- to 200-point seasons, and he caught the kids' imagination.

"KOHO seemed to be more of a teen and young adult market," Kaz continues. "And Canadien — it seemed the older player, that late-twenties-early-thirties kind of guy, he seemed to identify with the Canadien name. We started plugging players into the mix we thought made sense for each brand."

Gretzky and Bossy stayed where they were, on the Titan label. The rising new superstar, Lemieux, was assigned to KOHO, and Denis Savard of Chicago – then racking up Hall of Fame statistics with the Blackhawks (the team's new name after the 1985–86 season) – became the standard bearer for Canadien. Thus was branding refined in the hockey stick business. And Titan/KOHO/Canadien's market share steadily grew.

"It's now viewed that fewer is better in the stick business," agrees Steve Davies of Hespeler. "Look at Bauer/Nike. They do hundreds of millions in business, but have very few lead endorsees. Lindros, maybe Bure. That's about it. At The Hockey Company, they've got Mats Sundin and Mark Recchi. What you try to do is leverage your brand awareness at the retail shops that sell your product, putting up posters over the stick racks. You have posters of your three biggest guys – they're the guys who are really going to sell your product."

In addition to winnowing out the number of subsidized players, the companies also restructured their deals. Instead of receiving flat fees, players were rewarded for production. "So instead of Toronto's Rick Vaive receiving, say, a flat $20,000," says Kaz, "he'd receive a $10,000 fee plus bonuses for hitting performance plateaus of 30, 40, 50 goals. *Where* you played also affected your pay scale, especially if you were consigned to one of the many expansion backwaters that rarely reached the national spotlight. If a player toiled for a marginal team, he might get virtually no bonus unless he scored 50 a year." Today, some stick endorsement deals exceed $200,000. The oft-injured Lindros, still a Bauer/Nike poster boy, is said to make $250,000 a year. Leaf captain Sundin is in the $150,000 range, Philadelphia's Recchi at the $100,000 level.

The cost of maintaining an endorsee goes far beyond the promotional payment. In the case of Easton, the costs to make moulds for the graphite blades of its stars – Yzerman, Paul Kariya, and Joe Sakic – are so high that the company tries to get its lower-profile clients to use existing patterns. And for Bauer/Nike actually to make an Eric Lindros stick suitable for NHL play costs the company about $50. It gets back only $33 of that cost, so loses approximately $17 – a difference it presumably recoups in promotional value. "The difference between Lindros's stick and everyone else's is the amount of fibreglass," explains Bauer/Nike's John Hicks, assistant plant manager in Hespeler, "and the amount of carbon in the fibreglass to make it stiffer. You can't even flex his stick. Most people couldn't use it because they're not strong enough."

The value of star endorsement is unquestioned, but the marketing pendulum may be returning to the days when performance – not mere endorsement – was the ultimate selling point. "If you look at the way golf clubs were sold twenty years ago," says Mike Chaisson, director of global brand sales for Jofa at The Hockey Company, "there was always a player's name on them – Nicklaus, Palmer. Now you can't find anyone's name on a club unless he's invested his own money in it. Golf educated the retailers to tell their consumers that, just because Tiger Woods's name is on the club, it doesn't mean it's for you. If you're trying to improve your game, other things are more important: swing velocity, shaft length, and so on. The same is happening in hockey. If you

put the wrong product in the hands of consumers and over-
charge for it, you're not doing them any favours. And you're
not going to keep their business."

Chaisson points out another factor that uniquely affects
how sticks will be marketed in future. "In golf, you have
guys about six feet tall who are pretty much going to require
clubs of standard length and size. But in hockey, the specifics
of the stick are going to be dictated by playing style."
Indeed, the variety of roles among NHL players means that
position, training, and natural ability can produce a group
of similar six-footers who use different sticks. The lie can
be steep or shallow; there are heel curves (good for hard
slapshots), mid-curves (good for wrist shots), toe curves
(favoured by Europeans for handling the puck), and straight
blades (almost extinct); the face of the stick can be "wedged"
with an upshoot (for close-in snipers) or closed (to keep the
puck down). Blades can be long or short. And, of course,
shafts can be made of wood and fibreglass (better feel), aluminum (light to stiff), or composite (lighter than wood
and fibreglass, more responsive than aluminum). That's a
lot of variables.

Using player styles from a 1999 Bauer/Nike promotional
video, one can see how similar-sized players might have quite
diverse requirements. Take Pavel Bure and Wendel Clark
(now retired), both forwards, both about 5-foot-10 and 190
pounds. Bure uses an average lie to keep the puck out in
front of him; Clark favoured a steep lie to keep the puck
close to his feet. Bure's blade is long for control on patchy
ice surfaces; Clark's was short for touch and control. Bure
has an average-length shaft; Clark preferred a short shaft.

Bure used a lightning-fast snapshot; Clark relied on a heavy, accurate wrist shot. Two accomplished snipers, but using very different weapons.

Or how about Eric Lindros and Trevor Linden? Both are centres, both about 6-foot-5, both well over 200 pounds. Lindros prefers a blade with little curve, the better for making and receiving backhand passes; Linden uses a heel curve with a dramatic upshoot for roofing the puck in close. Lindros uses perhaps the stiffest stick in the world; Linden prefers something more flexible. Linden uses a number five lie, taking advantage of his long reach around the net; Lindros prefers a more upright number six for close-to-the-body stickhandling.

Small wonder that the order form for a Sher-Wood stick contains almost as many check-boxes as the SAT exam: pattern, lie, stiffness, shaft size, shaft length, top handle, curve, blade shape, fibreglass on blade, even paint finishing (neutral, black, other). There's even a box for the salesman to rough out the desired blade shape for the technicians at the factory. With an estimated $100 million U.S. annually at stake in the global stick industry – about 5 million pieces are bought each year – no detail is too small to ignore.

And with that much up for grabs, the salesmen must stay on their toes. "I'm not the only rep and we're not the only company," says Maillet. "You've gotta keep up, make sure they're happy all the time." If the players are happy with your company's product, perhaps you can gently move them toward a new product. And if you happen to catch the eye of a player who's waffling on his current model, well, new business is good.

"There've been some arguments," admits Maillet. " 'Leave him alone, he's my guy' – stuff like that." Indeed, with a franchise player, the camaraderie among salesmen can disappear altogether. "You see another pair of skates in a stall and it's 'Oh-oh, where did *they* come from?' So you go see some of his players, and next time he comes, he sees a pair of CCMs in his stall instead of his skates. It's kind of back-and-forth that way. There's a guy in my own company, he'll go into a room and grab other companies' sticks and draw their patterns. Send them out, make samples. I tell you, it's pretty tough. It's a game inside a game."

Want to start an argument in the hockey world? Ask: Which are better, wood or composite sticks? In the dressing room of the Mighty Ducks of Anaheim, you'll get a persuasive argument from one of the game's most gifted players. Paul Kariya sits on the training table taping his Easton Synergy, using the Johnson & Johnson tape he favours – "It's less sticky than hockey tape, and you don't get that black stuff on your gloves." His careful, toe-to-heel taping is a far cry from the ever-so-cool few strands employed by Bobby Orr in the 1960s and 1970s. "It's more like the wall-to-wall tape job Gretzky gave his sticks. The game's finest playmaker ever says, 'It enables you to pass the puck flatter when you have a decent amount of tape on the blade.' "

Kariya says you can't get away with a strategic strand or two on a composite blade. "With a wood blade, there are fibres in the wood that cause friction with the ice," he points out. "But with a graphite blade, there's no friction. It's smooth as silk on the ice. You need some tape there to give you the feel of the ice."

Kariya was the first NHL player to use a graphite blade and shaft; since then, composites have rapidly been overtaking conventional products. "Wood is going to become obsolete," says the Ducks' twenty-seven-year-old captain. "If you look at all the young guys now, you don't see a lot of wood. You see graphite and some aluminum. That's where the game's going. It's more scientific. It's where society's going, too."

In the 2000–01 season, Kariya adopted the new, one-piece Synergy stick; by season's end, more than 100 of his NHL colleagues had done the same. In today's hyper-speed NHL, this featherweight stick allows players a better chance to get off a shot before checkers converge on them. Even journeymen players can fire bullets using the Synergy. Elite goalies such as Dominik Hasek and Martin Brodeur were overpowered by shots from the Synergy in the playoffs. Some analysts think this type of stick could swing the balance back in favour of shooters after a long period of dominance by goalies. "We've got players clamouring to get their hands on this stick," Easton's Ned Goldsmith told *The Hockey News*, "to the point where they were buying them retail and using someone else's blade pattern."

The Synergy has been so effective in producing super-sonic shots that broadcaster John Davidson, himself a former goalie, suggests the NHL may have to curtail or ban composite sticks for the safety of players – the way Major League Baseball bans aluminum bats. Others speculate that the lightweight sticks (they weigh just 460 grams) are making reckless players more prone to high-sticking infractions.

It should come as no surprise to find Kariya on the cutting edge of hockey technology. From his Japanese-Canadian background to his spurning of the traditional development route of junior hockey in favour of U.S. college hockey at the University of Maine, he has always been distinctive. In the NHL, he has ignored the trappings of superstardom for a low-profile existence with the Mighty Ducks. Good as he is, his expected NHL dominance has yet to materialize. And reticent as he is, he's still considered the conscience of intelligent hockey.

For Kariya, the supremacy of composite sticks lies in their consistency. The average NHL player goes through 150 to 250 sticks a season and doesn't want to sort through a dozen sticks to find a few that suit his game. "I like the same stick every time," he says. "That's why I'm lucky to have found these. The stiffness is always the same, the curve is always the same. Weight-wise it's within one or two grams. Some players still like the feel of wood, but wood's never going to be consistent. Especially when someone's hand-curving the blade for you at the factory."

It's hard to argue with results. Despite serious injuries, including a concussion in 1998 that caused him to miss sixty games and the playoffs, he's potted 276 goals in his first six NHL seasons. "I think the biggest misconception is that you need a big curve to shoot hard. I remember when I was in college, I used a huge heel curve with a big upshoot. I went to the world championships that year. Most of the team were professionals, and I looked at their sticks and they were all basically straight. I said, 'Maybe these guys have something there.' My stick is basically straight now. If you look at a lot of the top scorers in history – Lemieux, Bossy, Gretzky – they had simple sticks, very little curve. They found something they liked and didn't change it.

"I haven't changed my stick for five years. I've only ever gotten mad at Easton when they've changed something. For retail they change the graphics. I hate that. I want exactly the same stick all the time. It's not a question of me changing what I want, it's a question of them making sure everything's the same. And that's easier with composite,"

Kariya has a keen appreciation of hockey history and fond memories of the wood sticks he grew up with. "My hero was Gretzky, so I loved the Titan sticks. They were great because they had fibreglass on the bottom. They never shrunk down and you could use them forever, which was great for my parents. They use my old sticks as tomato stakes in the garden. They're still there."

It's hard to imagine Kariya's composite model doing a tour of duty in a future garden. Or acting as a brace in a sun chair at the cottage, either, which is where some of the sticks used by Kariya's former teammate Teemu Selanne, now with San Jose, end up. "I have a friend who makes sun chairs out of old sticks," says Selanne. "I have one in my home. There are goalie sticks for arm rests, and the rest of the chair is the shafts of old sticks. It's really comfortable."

The Helsinki native prefers wood on the ice as well. He still uses the KOHO or Jofa sticks that originated in his native Finland. "Those graphite sticks," he says, "somebody slashes you hard, it's going to break. It's one of the things I like about wood sticks. When I find a good stick, one that I like, I can play five or six games with it. I don't break many."

"I started playing with KOHO when I was thirteen, and I still play with pretty much the same stick. I tried Sher-Wood but there's a little different feel to the wood. It's hard to change when you're used to a stick. I like the quality of the sticks – they're always pretty much the same. If it's the same pattern, there's maybe two or three bad ones, but the rest are great." So much for Kariya's concerns about consistency.

It's as hard to imagine Selanne switching to composite as it is to imagine Kariya converting to wood. It's also hard to argue with the contention that composites are the future. Besides Kariya, the Bure brothers (Pavel and Valeri), Jaromir Jagr, and Scott Gomez are among the many younger stars who use composites. "I think the Synergy is a great stick," says the genial Gomez, the former Surrey Eagle junior who won the Calder Trophy in 2000, and a Stanley Cup ring to go with it. "It's unbelievable what Easton has done."

For a generation brought up on space travel and silicon, composites are routine. For them, Canadian history is as much about the Canadarm working in zero gravity as about the CPR linking the Atlantic to the Pacific. Graphite and Kevlar are space-age components; composite sticks, spit out with the help of lasers and microchips, retain their production specs with astonishing accuracy. Wood, to these guys, is a retro flashback, the stuff of old furniture and cottage porches.

Not surprisingly, it tends to be older veterans who still use wood. "I'm just an old dog, I feel more comfortable with wood," said Al MacInnis. "I can feel the puck more, and it's been good to me all these years." Not long after making those comments, he too switched to a graphite stick. Many other noted NHL greybeards – including Ray Bourque, Chris Chelios, and John LeClair – still use wood-based sticks, but their numbers are declining.

If consistency is critical to NHL pros, as Kariya believes, why do half the players still use wood-based sticks? For one thing, say the critics of composites, if graphite is so special in hockey sticks, why hasn't it led to harder shots, the way it's revolutionized driving distances in golf or serve speeds in tennis? Players today aren't shooting much harder than they did ten, even twenty years ago. The odd player cracks 100 mph at the annual hardest shot contest during All-Star festivities, but the average speed hasn't risen much since 1993, when the competition was introduced. There are durability concerns about composite as well. As Selanne noted, composite sticks are oddly vulnerable to breakage from a slash or an inadvertent rap on the shaft. Finally, the cost differential between wood and composite means that most players are brought up using wood sticks. The cost of graphite puts it out of reach of many consumers, at least until a player displays the potential for a pro or college career. Such players must then be won away from wood.

"Is there going to be a point in the next ten years where composite technology will become affordable to the point where it will offer a stronger alternative to wood or fibre-glass?" asks Steve Davies of Hespeler. "Absolutely. But right now, the technology is still relatively new in the sport, and it's really servicing the elite level only."

Vital as the stick is to scorers, it's much less central to goal-tenders. "If I had to list my equipment in order of importance from one to five," says Hall of Fame goalie Ken Dryden, now president and general manager of the Toronto Maple Leafs, "I would probably place the stick at number five." "I'm the same way," says former Islanders, Kings, and Sharks goalie Kelly Hrudey, now a broadcaster with "Hockey Night in Canada." "My gloves, my leg pads, my mask . . . I'd put them all ahead of my stick." "I'd rate my cup as the most important piece of equipment," laughs Flames goalie Fred Brathwaite, stepping off the ice after a Calgary practice. "Hey, I just got hit in the ding-dong the other day."

Dick Irvin's book *In the Crease* has hundreds of stories about goalies. There are tales of masks, gloves, leg pads, goal posts, skates, and red lights; only one anecdote specifically deals with the stick, and that's former Islander Billy Smith waxing eloquent about its shillelagh-like virtues for clearing the crease. Ditto for Douglas Hunter's book on goalies, *A Breed Apart*, which deals with Georges Vezina's primitive sticks from 1926 and then abandons the topic almost completely.

No revolution in the goalie stick got press like Mikita's curving of the blade, or the addition of fibreglass, or the advent of composites. Curves were introduced on goalies' blades, too, but hardly anyone not wearing a mask took note. The blades themselves have grown by about twenty-five per cent since the Original Six era, but more attention has been paid to the bigger padding and gloves goalies wear today. There was the so-called Curtis Curve, which had a groove in the middle of the handle for a better grip, but it

STICK IN TRADE

was a washout for goalies who handled the puck a lot. There was also a blade that extended back past the hosel, giving the stick a sort of lop-sided, upside-down T-shape. That was quickly packed off to the Wile E. Coyote Museum of Useless Inventions.

For most goalies, the stick was simply a hunk of wood you dragged around the crease and used to block the five hole. "You had the heaviest stick they could find," recalls broadcaster John Garrett, who stopped pucks in the NHL and the WHA in the 1970s and 1980s. "They'd try to make the sucker last for months. There was even a time when they came up with this idea, they'd tape rubber over the sticks for practices. You'd use this rubber stick and you could hardly even lift it. I mean, it weighed a ton."

The shape of the goalie stick evolved around the turn of the twentieth century. At the time, skaters' sticks came in two models – forward and defence. Defence sticks had added wood on top of the blade and on the shaft for extra width. Goalies used the defence model. As the job of stopping flying rubber grew more challenging, a bright spark named Percy LeSueur of the Ottawa Senators popularized the idea of adding extra wood to the underside of the shaft as well, creating a wider paddle. Another of LeSueur's brainwaves was to carve messages into his stick. One pithy inscription proclaimed, in Latin, "The hand that turns away the blow." Alas, such classical references, like the name Percy, are nowhere to be found in more recent goaltending annals.

For much of the century, goal sticks got heavier while players' sticks got lighter. By 1916 the now-accepted maximum width of 3.5 inches for the paddle and the blade was established by the National Hockey Association. Because the extra width was achieved using the same rock elm and ash, the sticks, in the words of Ottawa's Hall of Fame goalie Clint Benedict, "weighed a ton." Swaddled in electrical tape, they didn't get any lighter. Coaching strategies restricted goalies to their creases in the pre-World War II years, and goal sticks were used almost exclusively for stopping pucks. They had to be hard, heavy, and long-lasting. (Photos of the day show goalies holding the stick in both hands; by the time of World War II, the familiar one-hand grip dominates the old black-and-white stills.) Until the advent of fibreglassing and laminating, extra strength came from extra wood, which meant extra weight.

Thrifty team owners were still squeezing the last use from wood sticks as late as the 1980s, remembers Garrett. "The trainers would say, 'Ah, that one's all right.' The stick had a big crack in the bottom, and you'd say, 'What do you mean, it's all right?' They'd say, 'Put a little more tape on it and it'll be all right.'"

With so little innovation in the stick, young goalies longed not for the latest wrinkle but for the status afforded by pro models. "The stick we all wanted around here was the CCM Pattern pro," says Dryden, who grew up in the Toronto area. "It was the stick the Leafs used. So you'd buy it at Doug Laurie's – I think it was the only place you could get it – and it'd be stamped 'Doug Laurie Sport' on the shaft. It had three or four thin blue ribbons around the bottom of the shaft.

"When I went to Cornell, in Ithaca, New York, the stick that was even more accessible and fascinating was the

Northland Pro, the one the U.S. players used. In any pictures of Terry Sawchuck or Glenn Hall, they'd have the Northland Pro. It was fantastic. I remember thinking, 'I'm able to play with a Northland Pro, this is great.'

"When I was with the Canadian national team [1968–70], playing so much in Europe, the big stick was the KOHO. The goalies loved it, they couldn't wait to get on the European trip to get the KOHOs. They had a stiffer shaft and they were a bit lighter. The Russians loved them even more than we did. Their own sticks were just brutal, as heavy as lead."

Just as the advent of the slapshot and curved blade changed skaters' sticks in the 1960s, the wandering antics of Jacques Plante and the poke-checking of Johnny Bower pushed the development of the goal stick. For a goalie to play the puck outside his crease, à la Plante, or to snake the stick out and poke the puck away from a careless forward, an art perfected by Bower, the stick had to be light and manoeuvrable. Such dexterity was next to impossible with the battle-axes used by goalies at the time.

Once again, fibreglass came to the rescue. Just as it had lightened players' sticks without sacrificing strength, fibreglass lightened the goal stick, too. Sher-Wood first wrapped the blade and heel of the goalie stick in the late 1950s; it wrapped the entire shaft in the 1970s. The added strength allowed for less wood in the sticks. "Sher-Wood was the lightest of them all," recalls Dryden, who adopted them when he joined the Canadiens in 1970. "They were unbelievably light relative to the ones before. What they did was bevel the edges so they were just as wide but not as heavy."

Today the edges of the goalie stick look like the gently rounded bottom of a boat, a far cry from the squared board used by Turk Broda or Bill Durnan.

Through the 1970s and much of the 1980s, goalie sticks were still principally made of wood. Faced with howitzer slapshots, protected by little more than felt and leather and goodwill, some goalies became adept at using their sticks to take more shots. "You look at Doug Favell and Gerry Cheevers, they were masters at waving their stick at the puck," recalls Garrett. "It was the guys who played lacrosse and had used the lacrosse stick to pick the ball out of the air. Cheevers, in particular, he'd stand over by one post in practice so he wouldn't get hit with the puck. And he'd get seven out of ten shots just by waving the stick."

The great change in goalie sticks came with the introduction of foam-filled cores. The technology had a short life with regular sticks, but it was ideal for goal sticks. Foam-filled sticks are dramatically lighter, and the fibreglass wrap absorbs shock. While the sticks are not as durable as the wood models, financial concerns are irrelevant in today's high-stakes NHL. Long gone are the days when part of the trainer's job was to nurse the goalie's stick through many games and weeks of practice.

As the speed of the game picked up and rules forbade goalies from freezing the puck, they needed still lighter, more manoeuvrable sticks to let them act as a sort of third defenceman on dump-ins. Puck-handling and passing became part of the goalie's arsenal. Ron Hextall of Philadelphia was the first NHL goaltender to use a curved blade on his stick; he wanted to optimize his ability to shoot the puck along the boards.

"Coming out of the net and shooting the puck are things I always did," Hextall told Dick Irvin in *In the Crease*. "When I was young, I used to get bored in the net. I used to skate around in the zone and behind the net. Then I started handling the puck. When I was twelve years old, I could shoot the puck in the air from the goal crease over the red line. I remember watching Jimmy Rutherford shoot in practice and I thought, 'Wow! He can raise it, even hit the glass.'"

The curve was quickly adopted by goalies around the league. But it required an adjustment in playing style, because a puck deflecting off a straight blade tended to skitter into the corner of the rink; with a curved blade, however, more rebounds came right back out in front of the net. The solution has been the paddle-down style of play. As it sunk in with goalies around the league that seventy to eighty per cent of all goals are scored along the ice, they began putting the longer, straight edge of the shaft – not the curved edge of the blade – on the ice to block close-in shots. This technique was better on screened shots, handled more deflections, and made it easier to steer pucks to the corner. Ed Belfour and Dominik Hasek were the pioneers of this style, one that's now almost universally employed in the NHL.

As well as curving his stick, Hextall also extended the narrow part of the shaft, giving himself greater leverage with his lower hand when shooting. Today, almost all goalies use the Hextall modifications. Fittingly, Hextall – the grandson of Hall of Famer Bryan Hextall and son of Bryan Hextall

Jr. – became the first goalie credited with an NHL goal (he was the last Philadelphia player to touch the puck before the old Colorado Rockies put one in their own net). In 1987 he became the first goalie to actively score in an NHL game when he shot the puck the length of the ice into an empty Boston net. "They dumped it in but it was to my right, and I couldn't get around to get a good enough shot," he recalls. "I'm a left-handed shot. Then they came back and Gord Kluzak dumped it in to my left side. I just fired it up and over everybody and in it went. I didn't think it was such a big deal. There were guys on our team who were happier than I was." Hextall also scored the first playoff goal by a goalie, into the empty Washington net during the 1989 playoffs (leaving him a mere 192 goals back of his granddad and 96 behind his dad in lifetime NHL goals).

Today's state-of-the-art goal stick is probably the Heaton that belongs to Martin Brodeur, who's won two Stanley Cup championships with the Devils. Having shortened the paddle, he gives himself more shaft for puck-handling purposes; then he made it as light as possible with the foam-injection process and refined the curved blade for handling the puck behind the net and clearing it out along the boards. Brodeur has complemented his natural skills to the point that he passes and shoots almost as well as some NHL snipers. He uses these gifts brilliantly, especially during penalty kills, and he scored against the unguarded Montreal net in the 1997 playoffs.

Talk to a modern NHL goalie about his stick and he'll mention passing and shooting, not stopping the puck. "I think that's the biggest change," says Hrudey. "It's the thing I had to work on most in my career, because when I came up I liked to stay close to the net." Scouting reports have led some teams to concentrate on forcing certain goalies to handle the puck as often as possible. Teams taking on Buffalo have tried to exploit what they saw as Hasek's puck-handling deficiencies; ditto for Dallas's Belfour and Detroit's Chris Osgood.

Who are the best-shooting goalies in today's game? "Do you mean a good shooter or a smart shooter?" asks Fred Brathwaite, now with St. Louis, who's scored goals in both junior and the IHL. "Brodeur has a real good shot, of course. But Jeff Hackett [of Montreal] is a real smart shooter. He's always making the right pass or shot to where it should go. Belfour, too, he handles the puck a lot – sometimes too much – but he's pretty good at making a smart play. I like watching these guys, because I'm trying to become a smarter shooter myself."

Goalie sticks, of course, have another important function. They have always been handy for intimidating forwards who get too close. No less an authority than Lloyd Percival's *Hockey Handbook* – hardly a text on goon hockey – talks about the protective virtues of the stick. Percival says, rather delicately, that the stick can be "used as a barrier to protect goalies from attacking forwards" and to "push off opposing players who may be screening a goalie's view."

"I remember when I started with the Islanders," recalls Kelly Hrudey. "Billy Smith used his stick to intimidate. So did Hextall in Philadelphia. If you were playing us or the

Flyers, you didn't try to wrap it around the post, you went wide because you knew that stick was coming out and it was going to catch your ankle. Billy taught me to swing from one post to the other, but I never did it quite like he did."

"All goalies are taught to swing the stick from one post to the other," adds Garrett. "You wave it, you swing it around there, you make sure that if the guy's going to come out, he's gonna have to come out wide. That'll give you more time to get over and make the save."

Smith was probably the most notorious axe man in the crease. Smith used an extra-long paddle ("three inches over regulation size," claims a rival) to clear the front of the Islanders' net as they won four straight Stanley Cup titles. "I just tried to give myself a little working room," he explained innocently. Tell it to the Oilers' Glenn Anderson, who received a vicious slash in the 1983 playoffs, or to Curt Fraser of the Black Hawks, whose cheek and jaw were broken by a Smith hack in 1985. Tough guy Tiger Williams was so apoplectic at the Islander goalie for axing his legs that he threatened to "punch Smith in the esophagus so he has to eat out of a blender for six months." Smith may not have won many friends along the way, but he won the Conn Smythe Trophy as playoff MVP in 1983 to go with his Stanley Cup rings, and he is now in the Hall of Fame.

Hextall earned notoriety with a nasty slash on Edmonton's Kent Nilsson in the 1987 Stanley Cup final (for which he got an eight-game suspension). During training camp for the 1987 Canada Cup, Hextall broke the arm of teammate Sylvain Turgeon. And a tomahawk chop on Jim Cummins of Detroit in the 1991 pre-season earned him another suspension, this one six games. Hextall claims to be sorry for these infractions, but says he was only protecting himself against forwards who crashed his crease. "The refs weren't protecting me, so I was going to protect myself."

Even Rangers goalie Mike Richter, not known as a hatchet man, used his stick on Tie Domi, then of Toronto, after Domi sucker-punched New York defenceman Ulf Samuelsson. "I was low on sticks," Richter deadpanned, "and I decided not to waste one on his head."

Not all goalies are inclined to chop down forwards who stray into the crease. Former Washington goalie Bernie Wolfe remembers being coached in the lethal art of slashing ankles by then-coach Tommy McVie. McVie wanted the mild-mannered Wolfe to be more like Billy Smith. One night, Wolfe decided to impress the coach by chopping at the ankles of a Minnesota player – ironically, Ron Hextall's father, Bryan Jr. – who was tied up with Capitals defenceman Yvon Labre. Wolfe took a mighty hack at the Minnesota player. "He doesn't budge, doesn't blink, he doesn't even get mad. Yvon is looking at me, so right away I start explaining that I hit Hextall as hard as I could. Yvon said, 'I'm proud of you for trying, but you missed him and hit me.' I almost broke his ankle, and he missed two games."

As a result of the damage inflicted by the likes of Smith and Hextall, the NHL in 1987 expanded the crease to a semicircle with a six-foot radius. Opposing players were forbidden from setting foot in the crease. Scoring plummeted – though too late for Hextall and Smith, who'd caused the change by swinging their goal sticks like the broad-axe men who cleared the Ottawa Valley in the nineteenth century. It was not the first time the dual nature of the stick – tool and weapon – would haunt the people who run hockey. Nor would it be the last.

CHAPTER 8

LAYING ON
THE LUMBER

What they worry about most is injuries
    broken arms and legs and
fractured skulls opening so doctors
can see such bloody beautiful things almost
not quite happening in the bone rooms
    as they happen outside.

Al Purdy, "Hockey Players," 1961

Marty McSorley is wearing a handsome blue jacket and a canary yellow tie, looking every inch the tanned Los Angeleno. He could be in a Brentwood bistro; instead, he's in the witness box of Courtroom 303 of the British Columbia courthouse in a grimy section of Vancouver. The thirty-seven-year-old defenceman, who started his career as a minor leaguer in Cayuga, Ontario, and ended up an NHL star in Los Angeles, is clearly preoccupied as he awaits inquisition by Crown prosecutor Michael Hicks. Over his 961 NHL games, McSorley served the equivalent of almost fifty-seven games in the penalty box – to say nothing of the multiple suspensions for flagrant fouls that kept him out of games. This bright September day, McSorley faces the possibility of a harsher sentence: a jail term for assaulting Vancouver's Donald Brashear with his stick.

In the dying seconds of a game against the Canucks on February 21, 2000, McSorley took a two-handed chop at Brashear's head. The blow stunned the big Vancouver enforcer. In falling to the ice, Brashear lost his helmet, allowing the back of his skull to smack the ice with a sickening thud. He lay bleeding and convulsing with a serious concussion even as McSorley bent over his unconscious body to shout some final obscenities. As a result of this act – caught from several angles on videotape – provincial authorities charged McSorley with assault with a weapon: his hockey stick.

What kind of man would do such a thing? At first blush, McSorley doesn't seem the type. Off the ice, he's a funny, handsome, engaging, articulate rogue whose leadership helped galvanize his fellow players in their labour showdowns with the NHL. But hockey is a fickle profession that rewards and punishes in extremes. In many respects, the incident came down to dwindling options for a player on his last legs in the big time and the price he was willing to pay for one more year in the spotlight.

McSorley is fond of telling the story of his father and the family dog. One day, the border collie heard something in a bush and rushed in to investigate. The next thing Bill

McSorley heard was a ferocious fight between the mutt and a coyote. Moments later, the battered and torn pooch emerged from the bush, tail between his legs, and found safety at McSorley Sr.'s feet. At a safe distance, the dog barked at his conqueror. According to family legend, Bill gave the dog a kick in the direction of the woods: "You yellow son of a bitch, McSorleys don't back down from anything. Now get back in there and fight!"

The gravity of McSorley's predicament is underscored by the cast of hockey luminaries assembled in the packed courtroom: NHL Players Association director Bob Goodenow watches with a disapproving eye, having questioned the court's authority to try a player for hockey-related violence; IMG's Mike Barnett, arguably the most powerful agent in the sport, is there to support his client; NHL executives, spin doctors, and lawyers cram into the front rows beside national media figures, eager to see if the courts will usurp the league's authority to discipline itself. The hall outside is crowded as well: New York Rangers GM Glen Sather, Vancouver coach Marc Crawford, and Brashear himself are restlessly waiting to be called as witnesses.

The most important visitor sits in the second row next to Barnett. Wayne Gretzky, whom McSorley protected on hockey rinks for a decade, has come to lend his gravitas to the defence contention that all's consensual in love, war, and hockey. The game's greatest offensive player (and soon-to-be-part-owner of the Phoenix Coyotes) sits forward, hanging his head at the grim details of McSorley's attack on Brashear in the dying moments of a 5–2 Canucks win over Boston at GM Place. Gretzky's "spontaneous" appearance, just as Crown prosecutor Hicks embarked on the cross-examination of McSorley, sent ripples of excitement through the court building. A posse of fans and smitten court employees have come to gawk. If ever a demonstration was required of hockey's grip on Canada's psyche, Gretzky provides it with his cameo.

Gretzky is clearly conflicted; a man who has long eschewed and denounced violence in the sport, he has nonetheless been the beneficiary of McSorley's vigilante protection. Not one for nuance, Gretzky will say he is in Vancouver to support the man, not the deed. But his own long career, he knows as well as anyone, is a testament to the importance of men like McSorley and Brashear.

For his part, McSorley had been suspended for the rest of the season and into the following campaign by Gary Bettman, the righteous NHL commissioner. McSorley wasn't the only NHL player to swing his stick at the head of an opponent in 2000, of course. Scott Niedermayer of New Jersey had directed a two-hander to the head of Peter Worrell (he received a ten-game suspension), while Brad May of Vancouver drew twenty games for stick work on Steve Heinze.

Meanwhile, Justice William Kitchen and the lawyers insist that the game of hockey, with its tacit approval of intimidation and fighting, is not on trial. But they're conflicted, too, for hockey's code of intimidation lies at the heart of the case. Even the prosecution must first establish that society has allowed hockey to be a world unto itself, with codes and thresholds of violence beyond societal norms, before it can prove that McSorley exceeded them. Paradoxically, the conviction of McSorley for assault in this case would be tantamount to an indictment of their own laissez-faire attitude in the wake of so many previous bloody episodes.

The Bruins defenceman had used his aluminum Easton stick to avenge the pummelling he'd absorbed earlier in the match from Brashear. The stick itself is never entered into evidence, although a few cut-ups in court security have a laugh on the gullible media scrum when they tote a bogus stick with an evidence tag dangling from its blade past waiting reporters. (The judge is not amused with this bit of guerrilla theatre and promises discipline for the offending clowns.)

Any red-blooded Canadian can recognize a hockey stick, of course, and the evil it can do in the wrong hands: Canada's flag, red on white, carries the same colours as blood on ice. There is no debate about the efficiency of the stick as an instrument of violence, wrote Justice Kitchen. "Every time a player uses a stick to apply force to another player, the stick is being used as a weapon and not to direct the puck as it was designed to do. Whether or not McSorley assaulted Brashear, he was using his stick as a weapon when he struck the blow."

Canadians also know that carrying a club of wood or graphite is what distinguishes hockey from other sports in the high-testosterone world of pro sports. In anger, a football or basketball player has nothing but his fists. In baseball, only the batter carries a weapon. But in the inflammable hockey atmosphere, the potential for a dangerous blow is always at hand. Any player can quickly, expertly, exact revenge by swinging his stick. That implicit threat imposes a responsibility on each player; the stick can thus be viewed, like nuclear weapons, as a mutual deterrent that keeps the game from spinning out of control. Former Rangers star Rod Gilbert once explained the cockeyed chivalry when asked why he had fought with Bill Lesuk of the Flyers. "He hit me in the head with his stick and he didn't apologize."

The men who run the hockey business have always insisted that mutual deterrence is what keeps the game from deteriorating into carnage. Similar arguments are made by the gun lobby in the United States to justify access to weapons from a BB gun to an AK-47. It's an argument Canadians largely reject when they see the cost of that liberty expressed in lost lives. Change those guns into sticks, though, and Canadians staunchly uphold the Don Cherry Code of Mutually Assured Destruction.

This fundamental enigma strikes at the contradictory heart of the Canadian identity. "Canadians love law and order," writes Robert D. Kaplan, an American, in *An Empire Wilderness*. "The policeman is a national symbol; Canada's society prefers collective heroes, such as the builders of the transcontinental railroad, over individual ones." Yet people who reject the American concept of the right to bear arms possess a primal affection for this tool of vengeance in their national sport.

Canadian protestations that they are a peaceful and friendly people have not always washed with others. "The troops with the worst reputation for acts of violence against the prisoners were the Canadians," Robert Graves wrote in his memoir of World War I, *Goodbye to All That*. "How far this reputation for atrocities was deserved, and how far it could be ascribed to the overseas habit of bragging and leg pulling, we could not decide." Graves recalled one Canadian soldier who was in the habit of putting live grenades in the pockets of German prisoners to lessen his workload.

In hockey, too, outsiders have occasionally held up an unflattering mirror to Canadians. "We always wanted to win," recalls Ulf Nilsson, the Swede who centred Bobby Hull in Winnipeg. "But the Canadians *had* to win. They'd literally kill you to win." Sometimes, the observations were comic. "I always enjoy being around hockey players," joked Bob Hope. "After all, I've always enjoyed entertaining our fighting men."

For confirmation of this double standard in the national makeup, look no further than Game Eight of the historic 1972 Canada–USSR showdown, the most glorious game in Canadian sports history. Before Paul Henderson vaulted to fame, using his Sher-Wood to beat Vladislav Tretiak, there was the other use of the stick in Canadian hands. Just before Henderson's historic marker, Peter Mahovlich waded into a phalanx of Soviet policemen, stick poised aloft like a mighty lance, to rescue Canadian promoter Alan Eagleson from the clutches of the law. The Toronto lawyer had run through the stands when the goal light failed to go on for Yvan Cournoyer's game-tying goal. ("Had I known how Eagleson was going to screw the players later on [as director of the NHL Players Association], I would have left him there," Mahovlich quipped years later when Eagleson was thrown in jail for fraud.)

Then there was the distraught Jean-Paul Parise, skating across the ice at the Luzhniki Sports Palace with his stick cocked over his shoulder, ready to deliver a two-handed blow to the inept Czech referee Josef Kompalla, who had

given him a dubious penalty. The referee cowered, antici-
pating a blow; Parise relented, having delivered his message
of intimidation in the service of his country's game. It's an
image Canadians have buried beneath the memory of
Henderson's unforgettable heroics, but it's no less emblem-
atic of Canada's hockey character.

The legacy of stick work in the early days of hockey is less
well known but no less bloody. When Odie Cleghorn of the
Montreal Wanderers was KO'd by Newsy Lalonde of the
Canadiens in a 1912 match, his rambunctious brother
Sprague used his Hilborn special to open a gaping wound on
Lalonde's head – a wound requiring eighteen stitches.
Spectators in Montreal were so appalled they insisted on
Sprague's suspension by the NHA (he got four weeks).
Sprague was later arrested and fined $50. (The epilogue to
this story also says much about the players' attitudes to vio-
lence. When the Maroons manager Charlie Querrie went to
bail out Cleghorn at the police station, he found the
defenceman shooting craps in a cell with Lalonde, who'd
been called as a witness.)

The venerable reporter Elmer Ferguson once described
how the Montreal Maroons carved up the Bruins formida-
ble tough guy Eddie Shore. "A long-reaching stick blade
tore open his cheek. Another sliced his chin. . . . Just at the
end, a Maroon player cut across Shore and deliberately gave
him a sickening smash to the mouth, which knocked out
several teeth. . . . He was carried off, and five minutes later,
his wounds temporarily doctored, he was standing silently

beneath the showers. Expecting an outburst, I said, 'Rough going, Eddie.' Through bloody, swollen lips he answered laconically, 'It's all in the game. I'll pay off.'" (Shore ended the career of Toronto's Ace Bailey with a vicious check from behind. Bailey's teammate Red Horner then used his stick on Shore's head, knocking him out and forcing the Bruins defender to wear a helmet for the rest of the 1934 season.)

Indeed it was all in the game, an extension of the lumberjack tradition of loosening up a little on payday. With money in their pockets, whisky in their guts, and a winter's worth of pent-up aggression, the timbermen and rafters usually ended up in vicious fights where blood flowed as freely as booze. The authorities often gave these delinquents a wide berth, and the "boys will be boys" attitude became part of hockey culture. Like the lumberjacks, rough-hewn kids from remote towns and farms needed an escape valve for their passions. Hockey and its cousin, lacrosse, became the only team sports that do not expel a player for fighting. The use of designated enforcers – who typically lack NHL-calibre skills – has become a staple of the modern game, an indispensable part of strategy.

While Sprague Cleghorn's outburst landed him before a judge, the modern courts have, for the most part, chosen a policy of benign neglect. But as the McSorley incident proved, allowing the NHL to promote violence ("If we don't put a stop to it, we'll have to print more tickets," quipped Toronto owner Conn Smythe) while supposedly curtailing it has been a recipe for stick-swinging incidents. The Canucks were publicly outraged by McSorley's actions, yet in one TV promo for the following season there were three clips of fights compared to only one goal. In such a contradictory climate, breakdowns are predestined.

In the most notorious stick-swinging episode, a 1955 duel involving Maurice Richard provoked a mob to trash the downtown area of Montreal. Richard bordered on maniacal when he felt that he was being abused by opponents intent on stopping his prodigious scoring. The NHL had attempted to curb his outbursts through fines and suspensions, often without punishing those who provoked the reaction. So it shouldn't have come as a surprise when, on the night of March 13, 1955, Richard lost it after being cut by the stick of Boston defenceman Hal Laycoe. When Laycoe dropped his gloves to fight, Richard wielded his stick, hitting Laycoe on the shoulder and head. When linesman Cliff Thompson pried Richard's broken stick from his grasp, the Rocket simply grabbed another stick and broke it over Laycoe's back. When that stick was taken away, Richard found a third stick and broke it on the battered Laycoe as well. He capped the performance by slugging the linesman at least twice in the face.

Richard was already on notice from NHL president Clarence Campbell about earlier violent behaviour. He was suspended for the rest of the season and the playoffs – the harshest suspension of a star player ever in the NHL. Tellingly, he was banished not for his stickwork but for punching the linesman. Incensed Montreal fans rioted at the next game at the Forum; when the game was forfeited to Detroit, they took their anger to the streets, lighting fires, looting stores, and overturning cars. It took a radio appeal from Richard himself to calm the city. Richard was never criminally charged in Boston; the Massachusetts courts were apparently content to let the league handle discipline for whacking Laycoe at the Garden.

The same can't be said of the next frightening case in the history of stick swinging. During an exhibition game in Ottawa on September 19, 1969, a young St. Louis forward named Wayne Maki checked Boston tough guy Ted Green from behind. Green knocked him down. Maki speared Green in return. Green retaliated by swinging his stick in the vicinity of Maki's head. Maki then landed a clear blow to the side of Green's head and "Terrible Ted" crumpled to the ice. His face began convulsing as he lay there. It's one of the most frightening images in hockey history: the effects of a fractured skull taking hold. Two surgeries saved Green's life that night. He missed the entire next season. For his part, Maki was suspended by the NHL and charged in Ottawa, but those charges were later dropped. (Ironically, Maki died four years later of a brain tumour, while Green recovered sufficiently from his brain injury to play another nine seasons of pro hockey and then embark on a lengthy coaching career.)

If hockey learned from Maki's attack on Green, the lessons didn't last. In one stretch of the 1982–83 season, Tiger Williams received a seven-game suspension for slashing Billy Smith; Hartford's Blaine Stoughton was suspended eight games for cross-checking Paul Baxter of Pittsburgh; Willi Plett of Minnesota received an eight-game suspension for slashing Detroit goalie Greg Stefan; Boston's Ken Linseman was suspended four games for high-sticking Toronto's Russ Adam; and Jerry Korab of the Kings sat out six games for a stick-fencing duel with pugnacious Dale Hunter of Quebec.

The next stick-swinging encounter that put the NHL and
the law on a collision course happened in Toronto in 1988,
when Dino Ciccarelli of Minnesota repeatedly slashed
Maple Leafs defenceman Luke Richardson in the head and
shoulder. Ciccarelli was charged with assault and later fined
$1,000 and one day in jail. Naturally, Ciccarelli called the
process ridiculous. "I don't see where these people are
getting involved in the hockey aspects," he said after the sentence. The judge disagreed, saying Ciccarelli's behaviour
was unacceptable and the courts would not tolerate it. Most
jurisdictions, however, let the NHL deal with the stick fouls
by itself – with varying degrees of success. Which was how
Marty McSorley ended up in court in Vancouver eighteen
years after the Ciccarelli incident.

"The unwritten rule used to be that you did not hit
anybody above the shoulders," recalls Stan Mikita, a ferocious player himself early in his career. "The other thing was,
you don't swing to hurt the guy." But with better equipment
came a gradual relaxation of the caution displayed by
Mikita's generation. The widespread acceptance of helmets
made some players think the head was no longer vulnerable.
Expansion also meant that players faced each other fewer
times and could avoid retaliation for vicious fouls they committed. (It took Detroit three-quarters of a season to exact
revenge on Claude Lemieux of Colorado for checking Kris
Draper of the Red Wings face-first into the boards during a
playoff game in 1996.) Some felt the growing influx of
European players – who hadn't been brought up with the
same code of chivalry – was also a factor.

Whatever the reasons, the results were clear. The increase

in concussions and eye injuries provided evidence of careless stick work everywhere in the NHL. And even though bench-clearing brawls and other forms of violence were decreasing, most fans wanted something done about the stick as a weapon. It was McSorley's poor fortune to be the one to answer for the public's disgust with stick work in a juris-diction unimpressed by hockey's Svengali hold on the national consciousness. His premeditated two-hander seemed to epitomize the lawlessness of the NHL at the dawn of the twenty-first century.

But why was McSorley alone on trial? Hadn't he been ordered onto the ice by Bruin coaches Pat Burns and Jacques Laperriere with the implicit instruction to even the score with Brashear, who'd been taunting the hapless Bruins throughout the 5–2 Vancouver win? Why weren't the coaches and managers who employ men such as McSorley and Brashear to bust heads also complicit? Apparently a sweeping condemnation of violence, one that included NHL management, was simply a bridge too far for the Crown prosecutors in this case. Such a widespread indictment might even sweep the Canucks into the mess, and that wasn't the point for a progressive but unpopular provincial NDP gov-ernment that needed an easy PR victory. Which was to pros-ecute a wilful, violent attack on a member of the hometown team, the Canucks.

So McSorley, the loyal NHL thug, faced the music alone. Video of the cheap shot had been broadcast endlessly, and the image of a helpless Brashear being taunted by McSorley left many hockey fans nauseated. He was an easy target for a howling mob.

Before McSorley arrived on the stand, the court heard from witnesses who tried to explain the quasi-chivalric, quasi-mad code that governs the use of the stick in the NHL. Glen Sather, a journeyman player who later fashioned the championship Edmonton teams with Gretzky, used an analogy: "Battleships that carry equal firepower provide a mutual deterrent." Role players – Sather's euphemism for fighters and intimidators – are in the business of keeping the firepower equal by confronting each other at strategic points in the game. "But it's dishonourable for role players to go after skill players. . . . Role players are usually my favourite players," he added with a sly grin. Understandable, since Sather had been a role player in his far-flung career. In the end, however, Sather was obliged to admit that while there may be as many as 200 slashes in a typical NHL game, "every player on the ice is expected to control his stick."

Canucks coach Marc Crawford explained that while role players perform unpleasant work, the work is necessary in a violent, fast-moving game. But he drew the line at McSorley's deliberate use of the stick to injure Brashear – a man who'd had his share of fisticuffs through the years. Crawford swore under oath that he'd never asked a player to go out and instigate a violent encounter with another player. (This self-absolution evoked skepticism from the hockey people and media in attendance.)

For his part, Brashear kept it short and sweet. The 6-foot-2, 225-pound winger said that due to his concussion, he couldn't remember the incident and that people in attendance that night knew more about McSorley's actions than he did. With that, he left the courtroom without acknowledging

McSorley. Clearly, bygones were not bygones in this case. (Brashear, perhaps uncomfortable in the role of victim, soon reverted to type and was charged with assault on a man in Vancouver; the trial is scheduled for late summer 2001).

In the end, the Vancouver show trial came down to McSorley's credibility under attack from Crown prosecutor Michael Hicks. Like a wrestler exposing the tricks of his trade, McSorley was masterful at revealing the unholy secrets of violence in the NHL. In calm, articulate fashion, the veteran of six NHL teams described the times when it was smart to fight, the times it was dumb to fight, and the times you simply did what management had hired you to do. Anyone who still thought that players fought out of anger, or as a release from tension, was sorely disabused by McSorley's clinical dissertation.

Hicks seemed to be the only one who didn't grasp what McSorley was saying. Time after time, he tried to get McSorley to admit he went after Brashear in anger, in a fit of temper, a rage for revenge. Calmly McSorley replied, "If I was so angry, why did I go after the puck when I first got on the ice instead of going after Donald?" Precisely. This was no crime of passion; it was a deliberate, considered assault prompted by McSorley's fear of losing his job as enforcer. He understood that his job hung by a thread unless he could clobber the swaggering bully who'd pummelled him earlier. He didn't need his coaches to tell him; his entire indoctrination in hockey culture pointed the way. A fight after the game meant an automatic five-game suspension, so the aging defenceman had just twenty seconds to get Brashear. And with a reluctant combatant sheathed in today's protective equipment, it was going to take something dramatic to entice the Canucks enforcer into a fight. In a clear, reasoned way, McSorley went for the one target that could produce the reaction he wanted: the head.

While Hicks flailed about in his questioning, Justice Kitchen did not lose sight of the puck. McSorley could still not credibly explain away how a skilled athlete could aim his stick at Brashear's shoulder and instead hit his head. Kitchen's summation in convicting McSorley may be the most damning thing ever written about the institutionalized hypocrisy of NHL violence. "Laperriere effectively directed [McSorley] to get Brashear with about twenty seconds left. This was really too little time to fight, but he felt himself pressured to do something. He found himself gliding in from centre ice toward Brashear, sizing him up for possible ways to confront him. Brashear crossed directly in front of him, presenting an easy target. Brashear was the focus of all McSorley's and Boston's frustrations. McSorley had to do something; he might still be able to start a fight. In the words of McSorley, 'It had to be an instantaneous reaction.' He had an impulse to strike him in the head. His mindset, always tuned to aggression, permitted that.

"He slashed for the head. A child, swinging at a T-ball, would not miss. A housekeeper swinging a carpetbeater would not miss. An NHL player would never, ever miss. Brashear was struck as intended. Mr. McSorley, I must find you guilty as charged."

Despite the finding of guilt, McSorley never paid a fine or spent time in jail. And while roundly condemned for his actions, he was not entirely abandoned by a public that remembered the days when he rode shotgun so that Gretzky could safely amaze. In his stoic acceptance of guilt for the entire hockey culture, McSorley was strangely ennobled. Don Cherry chided him in the gentlest terms, insisting he'd been wrong to strike out but that it was understandable after the gloating of Brashear (the real villain, in Cherry's view). Others pointed out that he was being made the scapegoat by an NHL that resented his vigorous work on behalf of the players' union during the 1994–95 lockout.

Judge Kitchen asked that people not search for wider conclusions in his verdict. "Some may view the matter as a trial of the game of hockey itself," he wrote. "If that is their expectation, my decision will be a disappointment. My only concern is whether Marty McSorley is guilty of the specific charge alleged against him." But Canadians love to have it both ways. We thrive on regional autonomy and decry the lack of a national identity. We want to preserve our ethnic origins while having an identifiable national character. We write love poems to winter but seek out the sun.

So we can forgive Justice Kitchen if, no sooner than he warned against larger themes, he invoked them. "That is not to say that the McSorley/Brashear incident should not prompt a healthy discussion of hockey and the role of violence in sport," he wrote. "This is not the first time the issue has arisen, and it will not be the last, but it is a time when debate can focus on more than a theoretical problem. The public can watch the replays. They can read the evidence . . . and they can decide for themselves. If this is a trial of the game of hockey, the judge and jury are the Canadian public."

In that case, it's a hung jury. Fascinated and repelled by the dark forces hockey brings out in us, we can no more abandon the McSorley who used his stick on Brashear like a demented Braveheart than we can accept the terrible consequences. The Americans and British have never had our squeamishness about what lies deep in their national psyches; they've always been prepared to act violently when times called for violent action. Yet even these nations are amazed when the repressed instincts of a self-professed peaceable people are unleashed. "Whenever the Germans found the Canadian Corps coming into the line," wrote British prime minister Lloyd George during World War I, "they prepared for the worst."

When Marty McSorley lifted his stick against Donald Brashear, he wasn't committing assault. He was being Canadian.

CHAPTER 9
THE COLLECTORS

A boy alone out in the court
Whacks with his hockey-stick, and whacks
In the wet, and the pigeons flutter, and rise,
And settle back.

Margaret Avison, "Thaw," 1960

Your assignment is to create the definitive symbol of Canada. To sum up, in a single image, the passions and predilections of a people drawn from over 130 years of history. Which symbol would you choose? A sheaf of wheat? A Canada goose in flight? An Inuit carving? The maple leaf? The fleur-de-lys?

If you were the executive in charge of iconography at Expo 86, you manufactured the biggest damn hockey stick you could. So it was that a sixty-metre stick made of Douglas fir came to stand outside the Canadian Pavilion at the 1986 world's fair in Vancouver. The massive stick was positioned against an eighty-five-metre flagpole bearing the fluttering red maple leaf. The installation was then erected at the Canada Portal SkyTrain station. All it lacked was a 100-metre Wayne Gretzky to flip pucks into English Bay. In a nation where even the mention of language or geography can provoke rancorous debate, there wasn't a peep of complaint about the stick as a symbol of nationhood.

"History is important," writes the Canadian historian Jack Granatstein, "because it is the way a nation, a people and an individual learn who they are, where they come from, and how and why their world has turned out as it has." One hundred and fifty years after the Mi'kmaq first carved their rustic beauties from a hornbeam tree near Truro, Nova Scotia, the hockey stick endures in every recess of the culture. It tells us much about where we come from and who we are.

It may even tell us why so many Canadians shoot left-handed. Like Wayne Gretzky, seventy per cent of stick purchasers from St. John's to Victoria shoot left-handed. This in spite of the fact that Gretzky, and ninety per cent of his fellow Canadians, are right-handed in other things. Americans, oddly, are the mirror image: seventy per cent of U.S.-born players shoot right. "It may be a cultural thing," says Mark Hughes of Easton. "It really is strange."

And not a passing whim, either; statistics kept by Sher-Wood over the decades consistently reflect this 70–30 split. Canada also produces a higher proportion of left-handed golfers (like Mike Weir) and baseball hitters (like Larry Walker and Matt Stairs) than does the U.S. "Maybe Canadians are just smarter," says Todd Levy of Ice Hockey in Harlem, an American-based community program. Thank you, Todd, but before we get too chuffed, we should bear in mind that almost ninety per cent of European players shoot left-handed – in keeping with the traditional 90–10 split in the general population.

Why are we so different from Americans? The simplest explanation may be that to exploit the full reach of a hockey stick when poke- or sweep-checking, you must hold the stick at the knob end. If your dominant hand (usually the right) is placed at that end, you have greater control of the stick. Putting the left hand below the right on the stick makes you a left-handed shooter. As well, a left-handed shooter finishes his follow-through on the dominant right leg, helping him put more force behind the shot and maintain better balance.

The playground suggests a more homespun explanation. In ball hockey, players take a turn at all positions, including goal. A left-handed shooter can hold the goal stick in his right hand, then quickly adopt a shooting position by grabbing the shaft with his lower (or left) hand. A right-handed shot in goal, however, must either hold the stick in his left (weaker) hand or else reverse the stick each time he shoots – an inconvenience that takes time. Young players learn to shoot with their dominant hand on top when they play goal in ball hockey. It's a cultural quirk from which Americans, who slide the dominant right hand lower on golf clubs and baseball bats, are exempt.

Generations of road hockey players – such as those at the weekly pickup match at Bannockburn School in North Toronto – learned how to shoot this way. Tossing their sticks in the centre of the playground, they also used random selection to draw up teams. One player – usually the best – separated the battered Sher-Woods and Hespelers and Bauers into equal piles to determine the teams for that morning. The fallibility of this method is never questioned; the flinging of sticks in the parking lot is natural law. From coast to coast, players are thus constrained from complaining about the company they will keep for the next hour or two.

The game at Bannockburn has endured fifteen years of Sunday mornings. A morphing roster of players have hauled themselves out of bed (the famous Christmas Day game of 1995 is especially savoured) to perform the ritual piling of the sticks. In the early days, the game was held on a tennis court a few miles away; later, in a schoolyard in North Toronto with a basketball hoop at centre ice (heads up!). But for the past seven or eight years, this schoolyard has been the Maple Leaf Gardens, the Montreal Forum, the Luzhniki Ice Palace of ball hockey. The spot is ideally surrounded on three sides by walls and fences that keep the ball in play. There are few avenues for a puffing, middle-aged slacker to "ice" the ball and gain a needed respite. Like a squash court, the looming brick walls toss the players back upon each other.

The roster has been diverse. At times, the gang has included Robbie, a podiatrist; Dave, owner of a stationery store; Alex, a Russian-born TV producer; Gary, a surgeon at a Toronto hospital; Ron, a comic-book illustrator; and Steve, a TV host. Sons and daughters have grown up watching the game from the sidelines; some have joined the game themselves. Tempers have flared (as Danny Gallivan liked to say), and the game's co-founder quit in protest over a nasty check along the brick wall of Bannockburn. But the tradition endures, and tradition is what matters most in this outpost of hockey. After all, Orr and Howe and Gretzky once played this way, with improvised nets, customized rules (blinding morning sun in the goalie's eyes requires a switch of ends every ten goals), and a lucky stick that seems to last all winter.

"I remember my father putting on glues and tape and hoping we could have a good stick for Sunday morning," reminisces Jean Beliveau, who grew up in Victoriaville, Quebec, in the '30s. "But if you broke one, it was considered a big loss. I would do anything to repair them."

"If you taped them right, they'd last forever," Howie Meeker recalls of his childhood in the Kitchener area. "If you were playing on the pond or the river, there's lots of times it was soggy and wet and your stick would get soaking wet. If you'd get them dried in the kitchen and then shellac them, they'd last all winter."

"We were very careful with a good stick," remembers Mike Bossy, the Islanders Hall of Fame sniper, who grew up in Laval, Quebec, in the '60s. "Just as soon as we were finished playing with it, it went in the cupboard."

Ball hockey is the bone yard of sticks, the place they go when the stresses of real hockey are too much for their fraying fibreglass and retaped blades. Being whacked and slashed by a weekend warrior is a last, inglorious station, far from the well-lit racks at the sporting goods store where they began life. There is no margin for deterioration here. The rules are explicit: no splintered or cracked sticks may be used.

And so the modern boys of Bannockburn treat their sticks with care, too, treasuring those perfect models: one with just enough blade to control a skittish road-hockey ball – but not so much blade that you can't get that natural lift from a shaved blade. One with a firm shaft, but not a log that sends carpal-tunnel signals up the arms. One long enough for poke-checking, but versatile enough that it can be employed as a goalie stick at a moment's notice. One that won't betray its weary owner.

Such beauties are to be cherished, and so the Sunday morning players try to coax one more slapper, one more backhand out of them, even if the wood fibres in the shaft are as hopelessly stretched as the ligaments in the players' knees. Even if the tape holding the blade together is now fifth generation, like the dreams of the player himself. The next stop for a broken stick is a snowbank, where the school janitor finds it abandoned on Monday morning.

Then there are the sticks that, through some miracle of preservation, avoid the ignominious snowbank and end up enshrined under glass at the Hockey Hall of Fame in Toronto. Or in the brick-and-linoleum splendour of Brian Logie's rec room in London, Ontario, surrounded by dozens of autographed photos, hundreds of other historic sticks, and thousands of famous pucks. To a hockey stick, Logie's basement is Valhalla.

It's fitting that, to visit this mini-museum, you take Highway 401 west from Toronto past the great old stick manufacturing towns of New Hamburg and Hespeler and St. Mary's, then exit at the Ice Palace, home of the London Knights, on the south side of town. Here Logie is waiting, a stocky, smiling, bearded, fifty-nine-year-old high school civics teacher. He's chosen the Ice House for a purpose; the aging barn has hosted training camps for the Boston Bruins and the Washington Capitals, and it was here, in 1967, that Logie first saw Bobby Orr, a crewcut rookie. When the arena is replaced in 2002, many of Logie's memories will go with it.

Not that he's one to brood for long when there's so much history still to be uncovered. If there's a stick of historical significance, Logie probably either has it or knows where to find it. He's recently come up with a hand-carved prize from the late 1800s, a short one-piece job with a hole drilled through the end to allow for a string. It's the oldest piece – for now – in his collection of more than 400 sticks. He's as passionate about those pieces of found glory as he is about the grey squirrels that noisily chatter at the front door of his home, waiting for the buckets of peanuts he spreads for them.

In his basement treasure trove, Logie points first to a blurry black-and-white photo on the wall: it shows a boy wearing a Canadiens jersey standing before the melting snowbank beside a rink. "You're probably familiar with the book by Roch Carrier – *The Hockey Sweater*. Well, I lived that. That's me in Montreal in 1947. I mean, if you went out to play without a Montreal shirt and hat and socks, they'd find you in the snowbank in the springtime." Logie was a goalie in those days – "before they wore masks," he reminds you. When he was ten, he moved with his family to London, where he played hockey, attended school, and worshipped his NHL heroes. "I've always been a collector of hockey things. That grew into collecting sticks. When I saw a stick,

I had to know who made it, where it came from, how old it was. It was a burning thing for me."

By the time he took his degree in social sciences at the University of Western Ontario, he was putting his expertise to work. "No matter what course I took, I tried to work hockey into the papers I did. I was pretty successful in the history courses. I did one thing on the original players' union, Ted Lindsay and the guys who were farmed out or sent to the minors and never heard from again."

Friends have suggested that Logie became a teacher so he could take advantage of the summer hiatus to pursue his collecting and research. He's the John Ferguson of cultural research, mucking in the corners, doing the unheralded tasks, unafraid to get his hands dirty at a flea market. (One treasured find was a book entitled *100 Things to Make from a Hockey Stick*.) He has buried himself in local libraries, defunct factories, and front parlours to find vintage sticks. With the sufferance of his wife, Nancy, he's wandered far and wide to uncover dog-eared waybills in dusty attics, stick patents in obscure government buildings, former factory craftsmen retired in western Ontario. And he'll share everything he finds with anyone who takes the trouble to seek him out. "Nothing pleases me more than to be able to help somebody," he says, running his hand across a row of prize sticks. "That's why I got into hockey sticks."

That "burning thing" now fills every nook and cranny of his basement, as well as the hard drive of his computer. Ask him to pinpoint a favourite stick and he'll rummage through the collection to show you his Bobby Orr Victoriaville model circa 1972. But before you get there, he's handing you a Frank Mahovlich CCM with its wicked left curve; a model used in 1965 by Jiri (uncle of Bobby) Holik with the Czechoslovak Lions; Neal Broten's Christian model from the victorious American Olympic team in 1980; a one-piece Spalding from the early 1900s, an aluminum stick with a wood core from the 1930s; Bobby Hull models from his days with both Chicago and Winnipeg; a Gordie Howe Team Canada 1974 special; an early Russian stick (with upside-down graphics) given to him by the late Flyers coach Fred Shero; and a Rocket Richard specimen stamped "Raymond Hardware" on the shaft. Each of these prizes comes with a story.

In fact, the real heart of Logie's work lies in the stories of acquisition, stories he's documenting in a book on the stick business in Ontario. While the Hockey Hall of Fame waits for materials to come its way, Logie has sought out his collection, bartering and sweet-talking. When Boston held its training camps in London, a youthful Logie befriended Boston Bruins trainers Dan Canney and Frosty Forrestal, the men behind the Orr-Esposito teams. Logie was working at a local sporting goods store, and he offered to trade favours for sticks. In exchange for collectors' items, Logie would drill new rivets on skates, adjust blades, or repair equipment as a favour to Canney and Forrestal. "They probably thought, 'Great, all we have to do is give him this old junk,'" he smiles. "Now I have more than one Bobby Hull stick, and Beliveau stuff I was able to get from them."

Many of Logie's European models came from haunting Maple Leaf Gardens when touring sides from Czechoslovakia or Finland or Sweden were happy to unload their

cumbersome lumber in exchange for the best modern products or a little customized repair work. The Knights of the
OHL were another source of sticks from up-and-coming
juniors who passed through town on their way to history.
"This was before the collector's industry became big,"
explains Logie, stepping around a box of game-used NHL
pucks. "I was usually the only one around asking for this
stuff, so they were a lot nicer about giving things away."

Logie's quest for memorabilia has put him in touch with
other hockey researchers, including Garth Vaughan, the
retired doctor in Windsor, Nova Scotia. Vaughan helped
found the hockey museum in Windsor to house the products
of his research; for now, at least, Logie prefers to keep his
discoveries where he can sneak down to see them in the
middle of the night. Together, the two men are trying to
apply scientific methods to settle the history of the stick.

"In anthropology you do what they call dating by association," Logie explains. "When there's nothing on CD or
in a book, you have to work on other factors. Sometimes,
further research will change your premise or your information, but you have to start somewhere. Now, you see, older
sticks are short. This is a Spalding from the early 1900s, a
defence model. Spalding sold sticks for years and years, but
they never made sticks. They were always made by other
Canadian companies. I have an old invoice from a place in
New Hamburg, and Spalding bought three or four hundred
sticks at about $1.10 a dozen. Spalding made two kinds of
stick then: forward and defence. Later, they modelled the
goalie sticks on this kind of stick. I know it's a Spalding
because I have some old Spalding catalogues and it's very

similar in shape and size. And the blade – see how it tapers at the front?

"The early sticks were paper wraps, with the information always on paper wrapped around the handle," he continues, caressing a golden-coloured Spalding with a lighter band of wood around the handle. It's from the 1920s. "I bought this at a flea market, paid $40 for it. It was in a bin and they had varnished all the stuff in it. I said, 'I hope you didn't clean this label,' and they said no. You can see from the patina that the paper wrap was on for a long, long time. For me, it was a tragedy that someone took the label off."

Logie's attention turns to a battered model with a bowed handle. "I was at an auction a few years ago, and I went wandering in the back yard. There was a pile of old wood that had been there for a while. This stick was sticking out of the pile, and they just gave it to me. It was warped, because it had had something leaning on it for at least fifty years. It wasn't deliberately curved.

"This one I got at auction recently. This is a Collegiate. Collegiate was a model made by Hespeler in probably the 1930s. You can see where the paper has been ripped. Unfortunately for dating sticks, the paper is just about always gone."

He takes another stick – the tattered remnants of a paper label clinging forlornly to the handle – from the four- and five-deep collection along the wall. "I got this recently from Salyerd's in Preston. It is so rare to get [a wrap] in mint quality that's been used. I've seen one or two in people's houses, but so far they're not selling them." Next he produces a tiny Spalding model from 1905. Though used by grown men, the whippet-like creation with its short, rounded shaft looks better suited to a modern tyke player. "They used to hold the stick in just one hand most of the time in those days," he explains. "They'd only put two hands on to shoot."

In assembling so much wood, Logie has become expert on the properties of the timber that once grew in abundance on the rolling hills just north of his home. "Unfortunately, the development has taken away most of the forest. What's typical there now is farmland. It used to be elm and walnut and ash and lots of species of oak and maple. Most of the white ash used now in the factories around here comes from the Adirondacks, not Ontario. It's a stringy wood, and if it cracks, it doesn't separate as easily into two pieces. When I worked at a sports store you'd always pick out the bat with the finest, tightest grain of ash. They'd last longer. Now guys in the majors want the biggest space between the grains. That makes it lighter, but not as strong. That's why you see guys breaking bats when they're getting a clean hit."

Through a friend, Doug Ball, a former photographer with Canadian Press in Montreal, Logie has met some of the men whose sticks reside in his basement. "Doug took me to Chicago a couple of years ago and we ended up playing golf with Stan Mikita in a tournament," he recalls. "That was one of the highlights of my life, playing eighteen holes and then having lunch with Mikita. I had so many questions for him he said his ears were red at the end of it."

Like all detectives, Logie lives for the moment when the disparate pieces of a mystery fall into place. While compiling research on the New Hamburg stick factory, he set out to visit Fred Rieck, who'd worked in the old Berger plant in the early 1930s. The route along Highway 401 to New Hamburg passes through the heart of the old stick industry, when almost every town or city churned out its own version. At one time there were many people who might have helped Logie piece together the story of this faded industry, men who were young during the Depression and who made up the backbone of the Canadian military in World War II. As he drove to see Rieck, Logie knew that that rich period in hockey history was disappearing. He was in a race against time to get answers to many of the riddles he encountered in his research.

To Logie's delight, Rieck had a generous recall of his days in the New Hamburg plant. He'd sorted the sticks into right- and left-handed models, he remembered, then stamped the paper wraps. He'd also been involved in shipping them all over northeastern North America. He told Logie about the various tasks with the sanders and the kilns in the factory at that time, and he recalled a labour stoppage by workers who complained of the cold during the bitter January of 1934 – a brave move at a time when a job was precious. Factory owner Clayton Berger quickly improved the heat inside the plant and work resumed.

Then the elderly Rieck reached into his pocket to pull out a small carpenter's notebook from sixty years earlier. As a memento, he'd preserved examples of the stamps he'd made for imprinting the different models. As Rieck thumbed through the pages of the old notebook, Logie's eyes widened. One of the stamps read "Maroon," another "Canadian," while a third was the autograph of the Hall of Fame goalie

George Hainsworth, who starred for the Canadiens and Maple Leafs in the 1920s and '30s. Logie knew Hainsworth had come from the New Hamburg region and played senior for the Berlin Seniors and Kitchener Greenshirts of the Ontario Hockey Association from 1911 to 1923. He'd even obtained a model of Hainsworth's customized NHL stick. The Hainsworth stamp in Rieck's little book was answering Logie's lingering questions about what factory had supplied the goalie with his custom sticks. The pad, with its greying pages, also confirmed that the New Hamburg plant had indeed made goal sticks before World War II. The stick and stamps confirmed Logie's supposition that the New Hamburg sticks had been shipped to Montreal, then home to both the Maroons and the Canadiens.

The final stamp in the book – a rearing, winged horse in red ink – was even more special. Logie excused himself to retrieve a stick from his car. "I'd long had a fine example of an old one-piece stick that had apparently been made as a premium for the Mobil White Star Service Station chain. It had always been a mystery to me where and when it was made. It had an unusual stamp on the handle, a red winged horse. I showed it to Mr. Rieck. The stick had been made in the old factory on Catherine Street in New Hamburg in 1933 and no doubt stamped by Mr. Rieck himself!"

When Logie said goodbye, Rieck gave him the small notebook. In his London basement, he produces it, opening it to the Mobil stamp. He holds the stamp next to the stick; the leaping red horses look as though they were stamped last month, not seven decades ago. A promotion made in the hundreds by a gas company is now one of Logie's most pleasing historical artifacts.

Fulfilling as that notebook may have been, it isn't Logie's fondest hockey souvenir. For that, he points to an unassuming piece of lumber on the wall. "The one I scored my only goal with. I was forty, playing defence for the Natural General Store Flyers in intermediate. It's indelibly burned in my mind. The puck came out to me on the point. I skated in and took a backhand shot. The only thing I remember is seeing the puck in the corner of the net. People say, 'What's the most meaningful thing to happen to you?' I say, 'That goal – I'd take it over anything.'"

Logie smiles when asked if people sometimes wonder about his sanity, dedicating so much time and effort to what are, after all, just hockey sticks. "Occasionally, when I'm excited about some old specimen, people say to me, 'I don't see why it's so interesting . . . it's only a piece of wood.' When my book comes out, that's what I'm going to call it – 'Only a Piece of Wood.'"

When Brian Logie began collecting, he was an anomaly. Why bother? After all, bent or broken sticks were as common as rain in the days of white-ash sticks and blades. But because today's graphite, aluminum, and laminate sticks break less often than wooden sticks, and because growing numbers of collectors are searching out game-used sticks, prices have got steep in the collectibles market. Gretzky Titan models from his Oilers days in the 1980s are a case in point. Though the

NHL's all-time leading scorer gave away as many as 700 sticks a year in his prime in Edmonton, few of the prized souvenirs remain in circulation. Jeff Mason of The Stick Rack in Calgary says it will still cost you about $2,000 U.S. for a Gretzky game-used model. An unused one will set you back about $400 U.S.

And where there's money, there's duplicity. When both Gretzky and Doug Gilmour were using Titan sticks in the 1980s, unscrupulous types would erase Gilmour's name on the shaft of the stick and replace it with Gretzky's. Innocents didn't know that Gretzky's sticks had their own model number – 1002 – stamped on the underside of the shaft.

Jaromir Jagr, the five-time Art Ross Trophy winner, is probably the toughest game-used stick to get among modern players. And for a simple reason, says Mason. "He doesn't go through a lot of shafts. In 1997–98, he only went through two. In that five-overtime playoff game against Philadelphia in 2000, he broke the shaft on his stick, then went over to pick up the pieces. The last one I had in, I sold for about $500 U.S., but I could've sold it 300 times over."

Some players create scarcity in other ways. Rod Buskas, a journeyman enforcer with Pittsburgh, Los Angeles, and Chicago, tallied only 19 goals (to go along with 1,294 penalty minutes) in his eleven-year NHL career. Not the sort of player whose stick you'd guess had collector value. "But he'd take two sticks to every practice," recalls Mason, "and then when the practice was over, he'd break both over his knee so no one else would use them. Rod Buskas! What was he thinking?"

Mason sells about 1,500 sticks a year, sticks he obtains

from teams, players, and league officials. "I don't deal with middlemen. There's just too many fakes. Even when you know the source is good, you can't always be sure what you're getting. I shipped some Richard Zednik models to collectors, and they all called to say the sticks had arrived broken. I'd never had that happen before, so I had them shipped back to see what had happened. It turned out they all broke in the same place, near the base of the shaft. Zednik's former teammates on the Washington Capitals had rolled back the tape on his sticks and sawed the shaft almost completely through, then replaced the tape, so the stick would break when he took a shot. They were authentic, all right – too authentic."

Gord Sharpe has just one collectible stick, but he believes the hand-carved model he's had since childhood is the world's oldest. A burly, smiling fellow, Sharpe works for the Ontario Department of Corrections and lives in Gore's Landing, Ontario, at the foot of Rice Lake. In the nineteenth century Gore's Landing was the embarkation point to the Kawartha region for frontier author Catherine Parr Traill and many other immigrants from the British Isles. A short drive away, in Fenelon Township, a Scottish immigrant named Alex Rutherford settled his family in 1851 and started farming. It was on his farm that Rutherford carved the stick from a hickory tree – making it ten years older than the oldest specimen in the Hall of Fame.

The stick looks like a gnarled shillelagh, barely recognizable as a stick, but Sharpe recognized it as soon as he saw it.

Sharpe was nine, and sitting on the porch of his great-uncle's place, when Melville Rutherford went rummaging through the cellar for the heirloom he'd received from his grandfather Alexander. "He came through the trap door with his long stick," Sharpe recalls. "Someone said, 'What the heck's that?' I said, 'It's a hockey stick.'" Sharpe's great-uncle told the boy that it had probably been used to propel frozen horse dung rather than vulcanized rubber for much of its life. The sixty-eight-year-old Rutherford wanted to give the stick to someone who'd appreciate it, and this wide-eyed kid was the one.

While the stick has sentimental value to Sharpe – he has a son of his own to whom he could pass it on – it wasn't until he visited the Hockey Hall of Fame in Toronto that he realized his prize might have monetary value. When Phil Pritchard, acquisitions director for the Hall, confirmed the age of the stick, Sharpe – a former Clarkson University player who went on to play a bit of professional hockey in England with the Billingham Bombers – decided to put it up for auction on his own Web site, hockeystickauction.com. He had appraisers look at prices paid for memorabilia items such as Honus Wagner's trading card, Babe Ruth's Yankees cap, and Mark McGwire's seventieth home-run ball, then calculate the scarcity of hockey sticks from the mid-nineteenth century.

Minimum bid? To Sharpe, one million U.S. dollars seemed about right, with a portion of the purchase price going to charity. When Sharpe's son Colin heard the million-dollar estimate, even he was in favour of selling the stick. Colin Sharpe went so far as to write Wayne Gretzky, a memorabilia collector, to solicit a bid; Gretzky graciously declined. "I could sit around here, worrying about someone stealing it, or I could put it to good use for charity," he said. So, while keeping the stick in a vault, he set out to find a collector willing to part with a million U.S., perhaps one who might then also allow it to be displayed at the Hockey Hall of Fame. He set the *maximum* bid at $5 million U.S. To encourage bidding, he offered up to ten per cent of the sale price to the broker who directed a buyer his way. Then he waited for the bids to roll in.

He's still waiting. Charity or no, some people in the memorabilia industry were skeptical. In part they were concerned that an older model might show up and render Sharpe's stick virtually worthless. "It's like the world's fastest man," Phil Pritchard told the *Ottawa Citizen*. "You're the world's fastest man until somebody beats you. Who knows what people have in their attics or barns?"

There were other complaints as well. "There's no real way to verify the date," said one interested party. Said another, "The price is way out of proportion. If a game-used Gretzky stick is only worth $2,000 U.S. at most, why should this be worth so much more?" When almost a year of waiting produced no results, Sharpe, ever the optimist, raised the price to $2 million and offered to donate the entire purchase price to cancer research. Still, the Web site remained quiet. An e-Bay auction in June 2001 proved just as fruitless. Sharpe remains undaunted. He told Mark Kelley of CBC TV Newsworld, "Buyers are proving daily that they are out there, and we're searching the globe for that special person to buy the stick and be part of one of the largest single donations ever to be made toward finding a cure for cancer. The buyer will be a hero in the cancer research field, and be able to store the stick in the Hockey Hall of Fame with their name and story attached. He or she will be making hockey history plus much more. Television stations and the rest of the media have already asked to cover the final exchange of the stick."

While he waits, Sharpe can take consolation from the fact that a lot of hockey heirlooms are going cheap lately. Molson Breweries sold the Montreal Canadiens and the Molson Centre arena for $190 million U.S. – about a third of what it cost to build the arena in 1996. And several Canadian NHL franchises have been shopped around for years without a buyer. Unless the memorabilia market heats up, Gord Sharpe's son Colin might be an old man himself before their historic stick fetches anything like a cool million.

CHAPTER 10

HOCKEYWOOD

The best carpenter leaves the fewest chips.

Old proverb

For most collectors, the ideal stick is almost virginal. Al Hehr, on the other hand, seeks out dead soldiers, the broken sticks abandoned behind the Zamboni machine or jammed into a rusty oil drum by the service entrance of the arena. Around Calgary he's a familiar sight in his winter cap and plaid shirt, a quiet, modest pensioner you might see hanging around the Father David Bauer Arena or near the Flames' equipment room at the Saddledome, a bundle of broken sticks under his arm.

Hehr takes the broken sticks back to his garage in northwest Calgary, where he restores them to life as benches, chairs, hat racks, toy boxes, and cribbage tables. An Al Hehr original, made of game-used sticks from the Saddledome, is a thing to be treasured in these parts. But money can't buy one; Hehr chooses the lucky folk who'll receive the fruits of his labour. His riotously coloured creations are his gift to the hockey world.

"I'm a carpenter and I like to work with wood," he explains, mixing Canadian pine varnish in his garage workshop. "It's the solid ash that I really wanted. Ash is better than oak for making furniture. It's a fine grain and you can smooth it down much smoother than oak. Oak has a coarse grain and it needs filler all the time. Ash is real hard, strong wood without all the pores in it."

Hehr keeps screws and nails in an old coffee tin, stubby pencils in his apron. His tools are perfectly organized in the workshop. "That plane up there," he says, gesturing to the rows of neatly hung tools, "that's a special straight plane that makes the edge straight, because of its length. It's what you used to use on doors, but then they came up with a power planer, which is a lot easier and quicker."

Hehr spent his boyhood on a family farm in Carstairs, an hour north of Calgary on Highway 2. The hills and coulees around Carstairs can roll for miles without a single tree – the Chinook winds blowing through southern Alberta kill off the ash, elm, and other trees suitable for hockey sticks – yet Hehr "always enjoyed working with wood. Always." With money in short supply, the devout German-Canadian Hehr clan had to make use of the materials at hand, and Al became proficient with the tools of construction. After Al married, his father helped build the young couple a trailer out of plywood and aluminum. When it came time to leave the farm, they hitched up the trailer and moved to Calgary to find work in the building trade.

"I got a job doing labour with Bird Construction, ninety cents an hour and that was all right. On the farm, whenever I went to work for somebody, hauling bundles or whatever, it was fifty cents an hour. Then they asked me to join the union – I wasn't much on unions, but I could get $1.35 an hour with a little training. That's how I got started in carpentry."

Hehr still sees examples of his carpentry in the booming oil town. "I did a lot of finishing – fitting doors, putting trim around the doors, panelling – and I ended up being the main door hanger in the union here. They blew down my work at the General Hospital [the city levelled the structure in 1998]. I did the doctors' lounge in walnut and now it's all gone. But there's a lot that's still there. I'll drive by and look up and say, 'Oh yeah, I was up there on top.' "

For thirty-five years, he adorned famous and not-so-famous buildings in Calgary, made a home for his family, and cheered the various hockey outfits that have called the city home: the Broncos, the Cowboys, the Centennials, and now the Flames. It was great fun following the likes of Joey Mullen, Hakan Loob, and Tim Hunter from afar. Who'd have guessed that, in his retirement, he'd have the city's hockey stars imploring him to make them a custom table or chair?

Inspiration came to Hehr during a minor game at a local rink. "I was sitting at the Twin Arena – this would be 1986, '87 – watching the guys sitting on the bench, their sticks up like so, all in a nice row. I thought, that sure looks nice, all the colours." He'd seen a local rink worker's attempt at building a crude bench from sticks – one that collapsed shortly after being assembled – and figured he could do better. "I talked to Pat Lawton, the manager of Twin Arenas, and he said, 'You can have all the broken sticks you want.' There were all kinds of sticks then. I threw half of them away, just kept the real good ones."

The first thing he made was a simple flat bench for the garden. Unsure of its appeal, he covered the sticks in brown paint. People admired his modest bench, but suggested he let the sticks' graphics shine through. When he came up with a design he liked, he resolved to give it to one of his hockey heroes. "I wanted to make something for guys like Lanny McDonald and Dougie Risebrough. We appreciated them – this was the time when the Flames were really shining, of course – so I started making up these little children's chairs with arm rests. They were ten inches high or so. I brought one down to Lanny at the Saddledome – he was so tickled. Then I went home and made one for Risebrough. And Gary Roberts. And Frank Musil – he wanted two, and a little table for his children."

McDonald, the mustachioed Hall of Famer who managed Canada's team at the 2001 World Championships, recalls the unexpected surprise of Hehr's handiwork. "They were great," says the captain of the only Flames team to win a Stanley Cup title. "I still have the bench he gave me years ago. Our family loves it. Some people waste away in retirement, but Al's making people happy with his furniture."

Word spread quickly about the benches. Made of brightly coloured Sher-Wood, Bauer, and Victoriaville shafts, varnished to a fine sheen, with their jagged edges smoothed and rounded, they were remarkably stable and durable. Everyone who saw them in the homes of Flames players or other hockey luminaries simply had to have one. Stores told him they could sell as many as he could produce (and were politely rebuffed). Hehr would go at his own pace, follow his own muse. All he needed was sufficient raw material.

So began the search for suitable sticks. He made friends with Flames trainer Bearcat Murray (and later with Gus Thorson, the Calgary equipment manager), as well as the maintenance crew at the Saddledome. Local arena operators were put on notice that he wanted their discards. A dozen years later, the many benches and tables and toy boxes in various stages of construction around the garage behind Hehr's homey bungalow stand as a tribute to his sources. The printed names of NHL stars who graced the ice at the Saddledome peek out from gaps in the seats of benches: Lindros, Nieuwendyk, Chelios, Sakic, Linden, Roberts, Iginla. The cross-braces on the benches are goalie sticks bearing the names of Osgood and Roy and Hasek. Sticks with their original blades intact are used in hat racks.

Hehr's furniture is cultural recycling of the first order, hockey debris lovingly fashioned into folk art, but the introduction of fibreglass and composites have drastically reduced the number of ash sticks he finds. "Fibreglass makes a stronger stick, but it's hard to work with because of all these edges." He runs a thumb gingerly along fraying shards. "You have to be careful how they peel – they're sharp – the fibreglass can come loose and get in your fingers."

For Hehr's purposes, laminated sticks are better than fibreglass, but only marginally. "They're strong, I can tell you that. I know from carpentry, laminated is always stronger. But it's a lot of work to get the veneer off and make the surface clean. That's what I use a paint scraper for. I scrape it all off and restain and varnish them." As for foam-filled sticks, "They won't hold a screw, so I throw them away."

Hehr selects a broken stick and scratches the top of it, across the telltale lines of lamination. "This is a very soft wood. I don't think it's any better than pine. For these thin layers they've got, I think it would have to be pine. Each layer is less than a sixty-fourth of an inch thick. That's what I've had to use since the solid ash ran out."

All these factors – the shortage of pure ash, the longer life of sticks, the composite revolution, the increased demand for used sticks – have conspired to create a shortage of materials. "I never believed it would build up to where I can never get enough sticks," he says, countersinking a screw for a bench. "Valeri Bure, he says, 'I want two more benches. And besides that, I would like three toy boxes.' How am I going to do that when I already have orders for six more and each one takes forty sticks? I told him I couldn't get enough sticks." Hehr falls silent; it's obviously tough for this gentle, Christian soul to turn down an NHL star who wants something for his children. "I can probably have one or two for fall. But there you go, it's just not enough."

The forebears of Valeri and Pavel Bure were themselves craftsmen who made watches in Switzerland before migrating to the royal court in Russia. Perhaps no one in hockey more deeply appreciates the time and care that goes into one of Hehr's boxes. "You can see the craftsmanship," says Val Bure, now with Florida. "There's love in how Al creates his work. My children are still very young. They'll be able to enjoy the toy boxes for a long time."

Hehr's unique pieces are increasingly prized, and he knows he won't be making them forever. He worries that the stick companies might try to cut him off in the belief that he's profiting from the work. (Any money he recoups barely covers materials.) There don't seem to be enough hours in the day. And his eyesight is not what it once was. "I have to be able to see properly so I can do the proper spacing of the sticks on the bench." Like the wood sticks he uses for his folk art creations, like the small-market Canadian NHL teams with payrolls in U.S. dollars, Al Hehr is fighting a holding action against time.

Bruce Saville can empathize. As a part owner of the Edmonton Oilers, the fifty-six-year-old hockey enthusiast knows all about small markets and limited resources. Saville has only to look at the basement floor beneath his feet to appreciate the scarcity of wood sticks these days. Hundreds of Sher-Wood PMP 5030s and 9030s stare back at this self-confessed hockey fanatic, a floor of sticks, end-to-end in his dream room, a tribute to the game he has loved and carried with him all his life.

Long before making his millions in telecommunications, long before he became one of the thirty-seven local owners who purchased the Edmonton Oilers from Peter Pocklington in 1998, Bruce Saville was an aspiring goalie in the famous Dixie Beehive Organization in Mississauga, Ontario. The Beehives' minor hockey program in Toronto's west end has turned out such NHL stars as Fred Stanfield, Ken Hodge, Randy Cunneyworth, and Brendan Shanahan. Saville never reached their level of proficiency, riding the bench through bantam and midget. "I knew I wasn't going to be an NHL goalie – in those days you had to be one of the six best goalies in the world. The seventh best rode the buses in Rochester or Hershey. So I went away to university and gave up on organized hockey."

But he never gave up playing; 2001–02 will be his forty-ninth season on the ice. You might say hockey has been part of the furniture of his life. Wherever work has taken him, from Toronto to the Canadian north to Alberta's capital city, Saville has always packed his goalie pads. "Have goalie, will travel," he chuckles. In 1999, he was called to be the emergency goalie for the Oilers – for a practice, at least. "I used to bug our president, Glen Sather – 'When do I get my tryout?' One day he called and said, 'Lloyd Whitney [one of the practice goalies] can't be here tomorrow, so it's time to put up or shut up. Be on the ice at 9:30 in the morning, and I don't want to hear any more about it.'

"At the start of practice, my eyes couldn't keep up with the puck, never mind my legs and arms. There was a defence drill where [then-coach] Kevin Lowe would feed the defencemen a pass. They'd shoot from the point, then come in and shoot again from the high slot. That was well into the practice, and by then I was pretty cocky." It was great fun. In fact, the story of the owner-turned-goalie made it into the notes section of Sports Illustrated.

It was on a road trip in remote Quebec that Saville first concocted the idea that he finally realized in his sprawling

Edmonton home: a floor made of sticks. "I went up to New Liskeard in Northern Ontario when I was thirty to take a job. There was a men's league there. One team had been really good, but they didn't have a goalie. In fact, the sponsor was the goalie, and they used to lose every game 9–8. I was looking for a team to play with, so I joined them. We didn't lose a game in the two years I lived there, and we had a wonderful time. We'd play all over the north. Once we were in northern Quebec–St. Bruno, across Lake Temiskaming – in an old rundown arena. The dressing room floor had kind of rotted away, and the janitor had made a new floor out of hockey-stick shafts – it was what he had on hand. You see it in showers, too, where guys have to make a grid to stand on. Anyway, this floor wasn't varnished or anything, but was it ever neat. I'd had the idea ever since to make a floor from hockey sticks.

"A few years ago, my wife at the time and I were going to build a house, a very big house. I said, 'I have this idea for what would be your card room, the smoking room, whatever, but it would be done like a hockey dressing room.' I started saving sticks and I asked Sather, too, and he always got me some. But sticks today don't break as often as they used to. In the old days, there'd be a hole in the wall under the penalty box and by the end of the season you'd get hundreds of them. They're harder to come by these days. I needed 800, and I had maybe 100 or 200. Somebody from Sher-Wood, the local rep, phoned me and said, 'Why don't you call up Denis Drolet, the president of Sher-Wood?'

"So I did, and he said, 'All you need is shafts? Well, we probably only need to print them on one side.' Anyway, he sold me the shafts, about 800 of them, for $2.75 apiece – pretty damn reasonable, I thought. The builder put a groove down one side of them. Then a new piece of wood was added on the other side to be tongue-and-groove. They glued it down and varnished it, and it really does look spectacular, doesn't it?" His pleased smile is bathed in the warm reflected light from his Sher-Wood floor. "The whole room is a dressing room."

To enhance the effect, Saville bought an entire set of autographed NHL jerseys at an auction to aid Aaron Moser, a local player left quadriplegic after a hockey accident. He added autographed pictures from Wayne Gretzky and Dave Semenko, a seat from the old Montreal Forum, benches, coat hooks. Presto. "Everyone who see it says, 'Wow, what a great idea.'"

Perhaps the crowning touch would be a few of Frank Gehry's chairs. The Toronto-born designer has become a leader in the postmodern movement in architecture in California, combining unexpected materials, such as corrugated metals and chain-link fencing, in his deceptively simple buildings. While Gehry, the 1989 winner of the Pritziker Prize for Architecture, has executed important commissions for the Guggenheim Museum in Bilbao, Spain, and the Loyola University Law School in Los Angeles, he has not forgotten the twenty years he spent in Toronto as a young man.

Inspired by the bushel baskets of his youth in the Kensington Market area, he created a uniquely Canadian style of bentwood furniture. Made from thin, laminated strips of maple, his chairs bear the trade names High Sticking, Cross Check, Power Play, and Icing. The accompanying table is called Face Off. The bentwood pieces need only a floor of Sher-Wood shafts to complete the picture. And at $900 to $4,000 apiece, they also need a millionaire such as Saville to afford them.

There's something familiar about the man on the mitre saw in the corner of his woodworking shop in suburban Montreal – an assuredness to the movements, a fineness to his touch as he turns the wood in his hands. Even at fifty-eight, with a carpenter's apron around his waist and a hint of grey in his hair, Yvan Cournoyer looks like he could still don his Canadiens uniform and skate circles around NHL defencemen. The native of Drummondville delighted hockey fans from the moment he took to the ice with the Lachine Maroons of the old Montreal Junior league in 1960, through a Hall of Fame career in Montreal that spanned 16 NHL seasons, 428 regular-season goals, 64 more in the playoffs, and the 1973 Conn Smythe Trophy as most valuable player of the post-season.

Cournoyer was thrillingly explosive, the Pavel Bure of his day. Only 5-foot-7, he had the legs of a lumberjack, dynamic pistons that propelled him past opposing defencemen as if they were stuck in cement. A wonderful photo from the 1965 Stanley Cup final shows Chicago's goalie, Glenn Hall, stretched to the limit as Cournoyer calmly tucks the puck in the open corner of the net. Black Hawk defenceman Moose Vasko looks forlornly on, Cournoyer having left him behind. The headline reads, "Hello, Stanley, It's So Nice To Have You Back Where You Belong."

That dramatic goal clinched the first of his ten – imagine – Stanley Cup wins with Montreal; for the final four triumphs, he was captain of les Glorieux. But that remarkable record doesn't begin to capture the Canadiens winger with the incredible burst of speed. Cournoyer was one of the players best suited to the large international ice surface when Canada's pros finally took on the mighty Soviet machine in 1972. In fact, the man who played in six NHL All-Star games was on the ice at the Luzhniki Ice Palace for the most famous goal in Canadian hockey history – Paul Henderson's score in the dying seconds of Game Eight that helped Canada defeat the Soviet Union. The image of an ecstatic Henderson leaping into Cournoyer's arms is indelibly etched in the national consciousness. Cournoyer himself had scored the tying goal seven minutes earlier; were it not for Henderson's heroics, it might be Cournoyer's name that everyone recalled from that series. Most critics felt that Canada – many of whose stars had faltered against the speedy Soviets – would not have won the series without him.

Cournoyer's nickname – the Roadrunner – said it all. "The two things about him were his incredible speed and his shot," recalls Ken Dryden, who played with Cournoyer for seven seasons. "He was not a good puck handler – he was a puck *getter*. He would burst into openings, and he loved to drive the puck. You could see the glee on his face when he drove toward the net."

In his playing days Cournoyer worked obsessively on his sticks, tweaking, grinding, rasping, bending, and blowtorching his Sher-Wood or Canadian to increasingly demanding requirements. "In the last few years he played he came up with a new stick," chuckles Dryden. "And he was so proud of it. It was actually shaped more like a golf club. It came down to the heel and was kind of set back this way, with an angle to it." Dryden's hands describe the club-face angle of a seven iron. "He had this theory that it would allow him to drive the puck better. But his shot didn't get any better. It got worse. I don't think he understood that the torque comes from hitting the ice first, having the shaft bend and then whip forward. Well, his new stick didn't bend, but he used it the rest of his career."

Cournoyer begs to contradict his old teammate. Relaxing in the back yard of his home atop a wooded rise in Blainville, Quebec, with the Montreal skyline in the background, he insists that he never changed his pattern after he came to the NHL and adopted the curved blade. "I don't think my stick changed from the start with Montreal," he says as his wife, Evelyn, and their fifteen-year-old son, Kurt, relax beside the pool. "In junior, we had no choice but to use the straight stick. We took whatever came to us. I was lucky, I always had a good stick. The owner of my team would buy me the sticks because I was one of the stars of the team."

Cournoyer used whatever came to hand to fiddle his stick, even if it meant taking his work home. "You weren't allowed to use an acetylene torch at the Forum. That was against insurance regulations, so I used to take my stick home. I'd bring it back to the Forum to do the shaping in the after-noon. I had to work the blade, because I was a right winger shooting left. I'd hook it in the heel so that when I received the puck it stayed on the blade. They were hard to make – the Drolets at Sher-Wood had a hard time making my stick. I couldn't play with a straight blade."

Cournoyer's statistics suggest that his stick worked just fine. Still, it had its critics. "My coach Scotty Bowman didn't like the stick," laughs Cournoyer. "Once against Chicago I scored five goals in one game. The next game, home-and-home, was against Chicago. I scored another goal, but the stick was cracked a bit. I said to [trainer] Eddie Palchak, 'Put it away for practice. I don't want it to crack on a shot in a game and miss a goal.' A few days later, I used that stick in practice. Bowman was critical of the curve, in front of all the guys. I said, 'I only scored six goals in two games with it. Is that not good enough for you?' He didn't say much after that."

When the Canadien brand came to market in the early '70s, Guy Lapointe, Serge Savard, and Cournoyer switched to the new model. "We were the first three guys with the company. They needed someone to use the sticks. I told them if you can do my sticks, you can do anybody's." And he sees vindication for his distinctive blade design to this day. "When I look around the NHL, I see a lot of my pattern, close to what I used thirty years ago. A little curve in the heel. [Vladimir] Malakhov used the same as I used when he was here with Montreal."

Had it not been for injuries, Cournoyer's record might be even more impressive (he had thirteen operations for hockey injuries). Back surgery finally ended his career in 1979, and it keeps him from playing with oldtimers' outfits. But he stays abreast of modern design. "I like to check the sticks, go in the room and check them. They're so light today. A lot of people don't know what balance is. It's not always the most expensive stick that's balanced. A good stick is like a good bottle of wine or a cigar – it's what you like, not what costs the most. It's like a tool. You must be comfortable, because you use it every day."

After his playing days, Cournoyer turned his passion for tinkering into a hobby. These days, instead of carrying a stick, Cournoyer is more likely to be wielding a hammer and wearing a carpenter's apron at the nearby Pro Ebéniste in Ste. Thérèse. The son of a machine-shop operator who moved his family from Drummondville to Montreal when Yvan was thirteen, he found that crafting fine furniture was like coming home. "I like to work with my hands, because I did machine shop my last two years in high school. My father was always working with wood."

The inspiration for turning his hand to fine furniture came from his Dutch-born wife, who liked to search the antique stores and flea markets in the Montreal region for fine old furniture. "I was doing little projects around the house, and Evelyn said, 'Why don't you take some courses in furniture?' Her neighbour had told her about this *atelier* [workshop] nearby. I went to see, and I liked it – I liked the smell. I thought it would be a good hobby so I took the course. I built a *secretaire* [desk] for my son, and when my wife saw it, she said, 'My god, it's beautiful.' So I took a second course and now. . . . I was there this morning. I'm building two pieces for my son to match the *secretaire* in his room. My neighbour at the *atelier* was kidding me that I smelled so nice. I told her it was my sawdust perfume."

The news that his old teammate and friend Jean Beliveau was battling cancer has focused Cournoyer on the importance of giving his post-hockey life meaning. Working with wood fills a part of that need. "I love it. I don't take orders, because then it's a job. I just have fun with it. The *atelier* is a good place to relax, I have my own spot, I have an armoire, and it's full of my tools. C'mon, I'll show you some of the pieces inside."

For a man whose career was filled with success, Cournoyer's stylish house contains relatively few mementos – his 1972 Team Canada jersey, his famous number 12 Habs' sweater, a few paintings and plaques. No stick from Moscow in 1972? "I'm not a souvenir guy," he says. "We didn't think about it at the time. We just wanted to win." His home may be slightly deficient in nostalgia, but it's full of the finely crafted furniture Cournoyer has designed and built. In the foyer stands an armoire in antique green and pine – a custom design for Evelyn. When a visitor admires the attention to detail, he demurs: "I'm patient for furniture, but I don't have the patience for the small things."

Then, as if to belie what he just said, Cournoyer swings open an oak door to the basement. The door is intricately carved with three cats' faces. The middle feline has its own swinging door to let the family cat come and go. The door clearly took many hours of painstaking work. Upstairs, Cournoyer enters Kurt's room to show his original *chef d'oeuvre*, the antique pine *secretaire*. "This was my first piece for my son," Cournoyer says proudly. "I have to make two doors to match it. I have to scratch it to give it that old look and try to match the base, the top, and the sides for an armoire and a bureau."

Next to this piece of Quebecois handicraft hangs, rather jarringly, an Eric Lindros sweater from the Philadelphia Flyers and a photo of the player who once refused to play in Quebec. Clearly, all is forgiven in Kurt's corner of La Belle Province. By contrast, Dad's photo with the Montreal Canadiens is tucked away in the corner of the room. ("At least he keeps his picture," laughs Evelyn.)

To illustrate the technique he'll use to age the wood for the doors to Kurt's bureau, Cournoyer produces a well-thumbed catalogue of Makita power tools that he covets, sighing imperceptibly at the sight of an impressive-looking router or powerful sander the way some men sigh over a *Playboy* centrefold. There are inked check marks to indicate the equipment Cournoyer plans to buy.

One of Cournoyer's favourite pieces is the humidor he built for his cigars. It sits beneath a colour portrait of the artist as a young hockey star, the blazing blue eyes and the powerful stride from thirty years ago captured in oils. He opens the top of the humidor to reveal a healthy cache of Cohebas and Combustos. "I'm not allowed to smoke them in the house," he says. "My wife won't let me. So I'd like to build a smoking room outside with some big Adirondack chairs that I made myself." And he flashes the trademark mischievous grin reserved for when he outwitted NHL goalies in his prime.

As the visitor makes to leave, Cournoyer has one last piece to show off. In a bin in the garage sits the famous

Sher-Wood with its violent-looking left-handed blade. As Dryden said, the heel curve suddenly shears back from the stick, like the edge of a tin can bent with pliers to get at the contents. Looked at from above, it's like an old airplane propeller, corkscrewed for greater lift. By today's standards it seems crude, but like a Highland claymore used at Culloden, or a scimitar from the Caliph's army, it has a savage beauty.

For a moment, Yvan Cournoyer – a middle-aged man in a golf shirt, far removed from his days at the Forum – considers the long straight grain of white ash in the blade. What's he thinking of? His 400th career goal? The Stanley Cup he accepted from NHL president Clarence Campbell? His moment of glory at Luzhniki? The back injury that cost him his career? He leans on the stick, bending the shaft. "It's important to have the right feel," he says reflectively. An artist never forgets.

Dick Irvin slides out of his car in the driveway of his home on the West Island of Montreal. It's a sultry summer afternoon, and Irvin has been golfing at his club, the Beaconsfield Golf and Country Club. A child of the Prairies, he's been in Montreal for more than fifty years as sportscaster, writer, and hockey sage. Like Jean Beliveau's regal bearing or Guy Lafleur's flowing hair, Irvin's lined face and laconic tone tell the visitor he is in the presence of hockey history. When the CBC needed someone to describe Rocket Richard's mercurial genius at his funeral, it was Irvin they chose as interlocutor with English Canada. When the Canadiens were sold to an American businessman in 2001, Irvin's was the opinion sought by media producers and researchers.

And why not? As a journalist, he was privy to the greatest succession of hockey teams the NHL has known: the Montreal Canadiens from 1953 to 1993, a club that won eighteen Stanley Cup championships in that span. The names are synonymous with legend: Richard (Maurice and Henri), Beliveau, Plante, Geoffrion, Cournoyer, Lafleur. Irvin's favourite club was the one he covered in the mid- to late '70s on TV as "Hockey Night in Canada" host with the late Danny Gallivan, and as play-by-play man on now-defunct CFCF radio. The team that included Lafleur, Cournoyer, Robinson, Dryden, Lemaire, Lapointe, Shutt, and Gainey won four consecutive Stanley Cup titles from 1976 to 1979. Irvin's convergence with a team that lost only eight of eighty games in 1976–77 was as fortuitous as New Brunswick's Ron Turcotte being chosen to ride Secretariat.

For a generation, Irvin's dry, unhurried analysis was the fitting counterpoint to the verbal hurricane kicked up by his ebullient sidekick, Gallivan, he of the "cannonading slapshots," "Savardian spinneramas," and "scintillating saves." Irvin was hockey's first purveyor of statistics on-air, a clinical analyst in a business full of pious gonfalons of gossip and rumour. If the Habs were the greatest hockey team on the planet, Irvin could tell you how they did it and back it up with statistics. Irvin's intellectual rigour, together with the team's astonishing style and heroic slaying of Philadelphia's Broad Street bullies in 1976 made the Canadiens the favoured team of artists, actors, and writers as well as Molson swiggers. In the years since, as les Canadiens became

THE STICK

a shadow of their former greatness and his broadcasting duties diminished, Irvin has written books, served on the Hockey Hall of Fame nomination committee, and been a helpful source of anecdote and history to anyone pursuing hockey scholarship.

Of course, Irvin arrived at his hockey pedigree honestly. His father, Dick Irvin Sr., was the coach of three Cup-winning teams in Montreal in the 1940s and '50s. Before that, the man in the fedora took the Toronto Maple Leafs to the final seven times, winning the Cup once. As good a coach as he was, Irvin Sr. might have been an even better player. The Winnipeg-raised centre once scored nine goals in a game – a feat that landed him in Ripley's *Believe It or Not*. Nicknamed "The Silver Fox," he was a star in the old Western Hockey League when it was considered the equal of the NHL, once scoring 31 goals in 30 games for the Portland Rosebuds. He left many legacies in the game, including his son. And the fence.

"Come on," says Irvin Jr., slipping his car keys into a pocket. "It's around back."

The back yard of Irvin's suburban home is long and pleasantly shaded, with a pair of squawking cardinals flitting in the trees overhead. Nothing announces "hockey" in this calm summer setting. In the northeast corner of the yard is a tidy vegetable patch, leggy tomato plants, and carrots basking in the July sun.

"There it is," says Irvin, pointing to a modest fence around the vegetables. "It doesn't look like much now." True: the wood in the simple fence is blackened and scoured with age and the ravages of Montreal winters. A casual visitor would barely give the modest L-shaped fence a second look. Even a close-up inspection of the fence reveals just a random letter here, the fine grain of white ash there. But for hockey archaeologists, this collection of stakes and nails is the Rosetta Stone.

"You're looking at something that's almost fifty years old," says Irvin. "My dad was a gardener, he liked to grow flowers, gladiolus. Back west in the summertime, he'd enter his glads in the Regina Exhibition flower show. He won a few times, too. I'm positive there's some Rocket Richard sticks in there. Doug Harvey . . . Boom Boom . . . Dickie Moore. My dad brought the sticks home from practices. I remember him unloading them from the car, because he had this idea to build a fence. He told the trainers, 'If you see a broken stick, give me first shot at it.' We're going back now to 1953, I think, the year they won the Stanley Cup.

"We lived in the Town of Mount Royal then, and I was playing hockey at McGill. Over the course of the winter he brought home I don't know how many broken sticks, and in the spring he made the fence. Too bad they've been painted, or we might be able to see the names of Richard or Lach or Bouchard on them."

Irvin leans forward, rubbing at the snow-blasted surface of the sticks. "I seem to recall the trainers would write the names of the players on the shaft of the stick . . . wait, there's something on there. S-T-R-O . . . it's hard to tell. . . . There was a guy who made all the team's CCM sticks in the '40s and '50s in St. Hyacinthe. They had his name on them, he wrote it in script – Jos. Choquette. That was his trademark."

Any vestige of M. Choquette has been obliterated by paint, wind, and sun.

"I don't think there's been any part of the fence thrown out. It's almost complete – my sister has a part of it in Ottawa – and it's been painted several times. It was redone by Guy Rousseau – he's Bobby's brother – he was a real good senior player here in Quebec. He's now a family friend. He played two or three games with the Canadiens. Assisted on the Rocket's 400th career goal. All the screws and repairs are his."

An aircraft headed for Dorval roars overhead, allowing Irvin and his visitor a moment to reflect. The modest use of such mementos speaks to the economics of people in the hockey business in those days. A fence made of sticks must have been a thrifty, amusing notion in an age before pro sports became an excuse to open your own bank. It's curious to think of a man in control of the cultural powerhouse known as the Montreal Canadiens taking time to plan a summer garden, collecting broken sticks from practice, ferrying them home through a snowy Montreal winter. It speaks of a time in Canada that will not come again. "Let me show you a few pictures," says Irvin, gesturing toward the house.

The pool table in Irvin's basement is covered with hockey history. There are yellowing documents, black-and-white photos, fraying newspaper headlines lying across the green felt or in scrapbooks stuffed to bursting. Like leaves on the forest floor, the collection has a quiet peace about it. "I've been trying to organize this stuff," he apologizes, sifting through the residue. "I know I have a few photos in here that show the sticks from that time."

Slowly, mementos emerge from his father's playing career in the early decades of the 1900s. Newspaper reviews of

Chicago's first pro hockey game – "arctic shinny," the writer calls it. "The fastest game Chicago has seen since the ember-laden winds of '71 raced with the fire department," enthused Gene Morgan. "The goal sentry is padded worse than some political payrolls. He is an overstuffed davenport on skates."

There's a column by Elmer Ferguson of the *Montreal Herald* on the namby-pamby NHL of 1926–27, entitled "Black Hawk Veteran Says Old Days Were Tougher." According to Richard (Dick) Irvin, "high sticks and slashing were much more common" in the game's infancy. "There was more 'cutting down' with sticks and skates" back then. Ferguson says of the greying Irvin that "he is not so grey or so old but that he stands in the first half dozen in the National Hockey League in goals scored, which explains why he is called 'Fox.'"

Then, most amazing of all, a photo of Dick Irvin Sr.'s teammates on the Chicago Black Hawks in the late '20s posing before a game against the Boston Bruins. In the centre stands the team's owner, Chicago's polo-playing, millionaire coffee baron, Major Frederick McLaughlin, and his celebrity wife, Irene Castle, who had teamed with her late husband Vernon Castle as renowned ballroom dancers. Raw Canadian boys from small towns in their torn sweaters, posing with the woman who was the epitome of grace and style in the Roaring Twenties. Tiny Thompson, Chuck Gardiner, Cooney Weiland, Lionel Hitchman, Dit Clapper, Johnny Gottselig . . . and Irene Castle. What curious friendships hockey has made.

Irvin studies the one-piece sticks in the hands of his father's friends. Without a magnifying glass, the manufacturer is impossible to identify. "Those sticks lasted a long time," he says. "But later on they started to break more easily. My dad had this idea in the '50s to position new sticks in the four corners of the rink. There was no glass then, they could just hand it right over the board. So when a guy broke his stick, he just skated over instead of having to skate back to the bench. It lasted a game or two before the NHL ended it. My dad said, 'Show me in the rule book where it says I can't do that.' There was nothing in the rule book, so the next summer they changed it. He was always looking for an edge."

With photos and cuttings in hand, the visitor heads out to his car. "People say it's not a sport any more, it's a business," Irvin says in his matter-of-fact, "Back-to-you, Danny" voice. "Hey, the guy who built that fence made his living at hockey for almost fifty years. For me, for our family, it's been a business since the day I was born. My dad was coaching the Toronto Maple Leafs or the Montreal Canadiens, it was his job. It put me through school. It's always been a business. Don't let anyone tell you differently."

As the visitor pulls away, Dick Irvin waves goodbye. Behind him, weathered to a timeless grey-brown, stands the fence of used Montreal Canadiens' sticks built to protect prized gladioli for the Regina Exhibition of 1953.

CHAPTER 11

SHOOTING GALLERY

All nations have such a buried or uncreated ideal, the lost world of the lamb and the child, and no nation has been more preoccupied with it than Canada.

Northrop Frye, *The Modern Century*, 1967

Ken Danby's ubiquitous print *At the Crease* may be the most popular representation of a hockey stick in Canadian art. A lone netminder, in battered leather pads and Freddy Krueger mask, crouches low, his chest resting almost on his knees. His body is tense, anticipatory, wary. He brandishes his Northland goal stick before him like a broadsword. Danby's netminder is a haunted warrior preparing to engage the invisible enemy yet again. The painting's heightened realism and its subject matter have made it an iconographic Canadian image, but it is only one of many artistic interpretations of ice and stick.

Peter Shostak, the son of Ukrainian immigrants, grew up playing hockey with his three brothers on a farm in northeast Alberta. In his illustrated paean to a hockey childhood, *Hockey . . . Under Winter Skies*, the vivid blues and purples of the winter sky and the golden stubble of frozen fields provide an idyllic contrast to the dank arena lights and grey ice of Danby's unsettling netminder. In person Shostak is a tall, angular man, but the dust jacket of his book shows a black-and-white image of a beanpole kid in flood pants, toque, and cinched gumboots, a brace of fish hanging from his mittened hand. It's not hard to see the boy of the paintings in the middle-aged man.

Shostak's paintings and prose stir vivid memories in any child who watched in wonderment, waiting his turn to grab a stick and play with the big kids. The painting *The Boys Will Be Getting New Hockey Sticks for Christmas* shows a frozen pond; four young brothers in their boots playing shinny on the ice, accompanied by a family dog; the brownish-red barn and tractor; the gold-and-blue Alberta sky of late afternoon in February. The movements of the boys are constrained by a handmade rink, which shrinks after each successive snowfall.

In the commentary accompanying another painting, *This Should Make a Good Hockey Stick*, Shostak recalls watching the big boys play on the flooded pond at school and realizing he was finally old enough to fashion a stick and join their game. "Armed with an axe and an idea [of] what a stick looked like, it was time for me to go shopping in the willow bushes for my first hockey stick. After sizing up what must have been a hundred or more potential sticks, I managed to cut one free from the snow and frozen ground. Back in the warmth of the farmhouse kitchen, I carefully peeled the bark and trimmed both ends to the correct length. Yes, my hockey stick was heavy, and maybe it could have a more pronounced bend for the blade, but it was just what I needed to claim a corner of the hockey rink." The painting shows a young boy in his fur-collared coat harvesting a stick from the snowy forest with his Boy Scout hatchet. Hacking out the sapling, he's asserting his place in the game.

Using his hand-carved stick, young Shostak gains respect and self-esteem on the ice, actually getting to touch the puck on occasion. With his elevated status in the schoolyard games, however, comes the need for a stick befitting his new place. "In Grade Three," he writes, "using a discarded hockey stick handle and a piece of plywood for the blade, I made my first, almost real-looking, stick. The biggest challenge was securely attaching the blade to the handle. I had observed the homemade efforts of the older boys and concluded that a piece of tin from the lid of a sardine can, shaped around the heel of the stick and blade and nailed through with thin blue shingle nails, was probably the best solution. A layer of carefully applied black hockey tape strengthened this crucial joint and gave the stick a store-bought look.

"My first homemade hockey stick had a much shorter life span than the time it took to make it. My arrival at the schoolyard rink, proudly displaying my carpentry skills neatly wrapped in black tape, did not go unnoticed. The stick became the target for one of the bigger boys who delighted at the first opportunity to give it a whack. I spent the rest of the game holding back tears and hoping my damaged stick would somehow heal or, at least, stay in one piece until the teacher rang the school bell."

In Shostak's work, the willow sticks and tin-can blades mark the intersection between alienation and acceptance, the creative starting point where imagination begins and the intricate patterns of passing and shooting make their mark on the ice like swirls of paint upon canvas. "May your skates always be sharp and the ice smooth," he writes as an inscription to the book. If the Original Six NHL teams evoke the golden age of professional hockey in the 1950s and '60s, Shostak's paintings evoke a parallel hockey universe, kids dreaming that the pond they're skating on is the ice at Maple Leaf Gardens, the willow branch in their hands a mighty, custom-made stick.

A bitter January wind off Lake Ontario whips the face of Michael Davey as he propels his bicycle along the frozen paths of Ward's Island. "That's where we played last week," he shouts, pointing to a frozen lagoon. "The ice was so clear you could see the bubbles to a foot or two deep. During Christmas, the ice was good enough that we could play right on the harbour."

Because of a thaw, Davey's outdoor "arena" is now a churning bouillabaisse of ice chunks and frozen flotsam at the foot of Toronto's towering skyline. In a few months, the islands will be swarmed by tourists and sunbathers, the harbour jammed with sailboats, ferries, and lumbering Great Lakes freighters full of ore from Thunder Bay and sugar from

Cuba. But now, in the slate-grey smog of Toronto winter, Davey and his artist friends on the islands keep the pristine nature of the game alive, playing shinny on deserted lagoons and inlets. Having lived since boyhood in this community where the nineteenth and twenty-first centuries collide, he knows where to find the good ice. "When there's a real cold winter, you can get a breakaway clear over the frozen bay to the Royal Canadian Yacht Club," he laughs, steering past puddles on the path. In the distance, a white speck looms by the lakeside – the RCYC. Now, that's a breakaway!

For Davey, the hockey stick has taken on concrete form. A noted sculptor, he has already had an exhibition of suspended hockey sticks twirling like propellers from the ceiling, with dozens of pucks spread on the floor. Now he's created a series of three granite sticks, a tribute to the Canadian game and the Canadian Shield. "If you think of the Shield, it makes up eighty per cent of our country," he says, parking his bike in a melting snowdrift. "I kept thinking of the zones within the Shield, like Slave and Grenville and Labrador. I wanted to make grand sticks from those zones of geography. Come on in, I'll introduce you to Alistair and show you the vitrines we're building."

The rangy, bearded Davey met his pal Alistair Dickson while teaching at the Edinburgh School of Art in the '70s. Davey had been a wandering hockey hacker, exploring the world, when he landed a teaching position in the Scottish capital. He has a wonderfully open, naive quality that allows him to engage strangers on just about any topic. For four years, he indoctrinated Dickson in the sacred art of hockey, which had been exported to Britain via Canadian servicemen in the world wars. Years later, after Davey had taken up a teaching post at York University in Toronto, Dickson came for a visit. He never left. He married a local girl and started a family. Now he lives on the Island as well.

As Davey enters the workshop, Dickson is labouring on the maple and glass vitrines that will house the granite stick exhibit at the Drabinsky Gallery in the Yorkville district of Toronto. "We chose maple as the wood for the cabinets because of its significance in Canada," says Davey, as his friend sands the maple to a papery smoothness. Dickson works quietly as Davey's words spill out in torrents; he likens his creative drive in designing the granite sticks to that of a Lafleur or a Richard driving to the net – "They were creative all the time, they had the vitality, the urge to play. They were totally inspired with a stick in their hand. I wanted to find a way to express that."

Aren't the refined world of art and the holy hell of hockey antithetical? Davey recalls that it was "Hockey Night in Canada" – that bastion of crewcuts and clichés – that sparked his interest in merging hockey with art. "One of the best shows I ever saw was Ward Cornell interviewing Frank Mahovlich on the Group of Seven," he recalls, as Dickson brews tea on the hot plate. "Frank owns Group of Seven, and he talked eloquently about his paintings. For someone from a Croatian-Canadian background, art was probably a luxury. It would have been more useful to have a trade. I loved his unease talking about it, but his assuredness at the same time. He wasn't showing off.

"Well, I saw him years later at the Art Gallery of Ontario. I told him I'd seen the piece on 'Hockey Night' about his interest in the Group. He laughed and said no one else had ever remembered it. I told him I thought it had been wonderful. He was framing some van Gogh at the time. He and his wife had been in southern France, looking at the places where van Gogh had done his paintings. I said, 'I think you should maybe frame it with a hockey stick.' He said he preferred something more neutral. He was right, of course, but I thought it was the sort of thing I'd like to do.'"

Davey's chance to incorporate the stick into his art came with an invitation to submit a sculpture for an exhibition on the Canadian Shield. He'd just finished a wall sculpture entitled *Between a Rock and a Hard Place* – a piece containing 450 pieces of granite, meant to illustrate the difficulties the Islanders had had keeping their homes from demolition by the Toronto Parks department. "I was walking on Hanlon's Beach, seeing granite pieces in the sand and in the water. And I thought, 'I'll make a granite hockey stick.' In my mind, it said Canadian Shield. The intuition came from my *Hard Place* sculpture and the barriers it pointed out. Play is where you remove the barriers."

The inspiration eventually took the form of a goalie stick made of granite with the words "Canadian Shield" carved in the paddle. Davey decided to include regular sticks as well. In each he would use a different mix of granites; each stick would have its own inscription describing the connections among art and hockey and the igneous formations that form the spine of Canada. The Wisconsin ice age distributed Canadian stone like junk mail across the top half of the North American continent. Quebec diamonds ended up in the U.S. Midwest, red jaspers in the upper Midwest, and sandstone across a broad arc from New England to the Rockies. Erratics carried from Canada litter American history: some say the Mayflower Rock started its life on the shores of the St. Lawrence River.

But it's the striking forms of Canadian granite that form the greatest endowment to American geology. Quebec's granite has long provided beautiful stone to the nation's most famous structures, and its American neighbour, Vermont, calls itself the Granite State. Each sample of the holocrystalline, quartz-bearing plutonic rock tells a story. In the swirls of schlieren and chips of biotite and hornblende lie the footnotes to a molten history written long before man emerged. The earth's elemental potassium, sodium, and calcium baked enormous cookies of stone millions of years ago in temperatures of more a thousand degrees Celsius, then wrapped them up in igneous, metamorphic, or sedimentary rock. What we know as granite is a common commercial stone; real granite is much scarcer. The many types of sandstone are the most utilitarian form of granite. It is a chemical dance of zircon, apatite, and titanite in the quartz stew that makes the finest granite special.

"Granite is so beautiful," says Davey, holding a sample. "This is ordinary white granite – you see a lot of it in the streets and in buildings. Look . . . there's even a little gold running through this sample." Davey picks up another sample, weighing it in both hands. "This is black granite – it's in demand in Italy these days. The sculptors and architects there can't get enough of it."

Davey wanted his granite sticks to be as close to the real thing as possible, right down to left- and right-handed curves on the blades. "I'm trained in stone carving," he says, "but I can't fabricate in stone." So he went to Smith Monument in Toronto, an Aberdonian firm that set up in Canada in the first decade of the twentieth century. The alliance of Scottish craftsmen with a game that has been greatly influenced by Scots (from "Bonnie Prince" Charley Raynor to Andy Bathgate to Al MacInnis) seemed fitting. "It's funny how all the nationalities that came here from the British Isles picked up the stick. Howe, Shanahan, McDonald . . . there's always been that great Irish Scottish thing in the game. The sons of immigrants became Canadians with sticks in their hands, but with the old country underlying it all."

The Smiths became captivated by Davey's idea of granite sticks. Cutting and sandblasting them to his specifications, however, turned out to be expensive – almost $2,000 a stick. And the technical challenge of emulating the thin edges of the blades was almost insurmountable. The samples either broke or cracked when reduced to the actual dimensions of a stick. Smith Monument eventually subcontracted the Europa Granite Company in Beebe, Quebec – a stone's throw, as it were, from the Sher-Wood and CCM stick factories in the Eastern Townships – to finish casting the sticks. "You had Quebec artisans talking to Ontario monument people about this project," laughs Davey. "It was perfect. Smith asked them if they had enough hockey sticks to complete the job. They said, 'Don't send us sticks, we have so many around here already!'"

When the granite sticks were finally done – the player's stick weighs about eight and a half pounds, the goalie stick about ten – it was time to inscribe each with a message.

"Canadian Shield" had already been decided on as the inscription for the goalie stick, a Rideau Red granite blade with a shaft of Prairie Green. For the right-handed stick, David decided on a quote from Northrop Frye: "Play is the barrier that separates art and savagery." On the other side of the stick is the French translation: "*Le jeu est la barrière qui sépare l'art et la sauvagerie.*" The stick's blade is made of Labrador Black, the shaft of Laurentine Pink.

"When you put a stick up against a wall in the studio, it finds its way into people's hands." Davey's fingers open wide to express the magnetic attraction. "Sometimes it's as a creative tool, sometimes as a weapon. That's where I like the idea of the stick as a barrier between art and savagery. The stick finds Canadians at their most dynamic with both art and violence."

For the third stick, Davey chose a quote from the Austrian scientist and philosopher Arthur Koestler: "The degree of playfulness in our action decreases in proportion to the exploratory drive as adulterated by other drives." (The lengthy quote crawls down the shaft into the blade of the stick; that created problems in carving the letters without cracking the shaft.) This stick has a blade of Mahogany Ontario and Gaelic Green granites.

Only a shortage of funds has kept Davey from exploring his theme further. "I want to do a straight-bladed stick to round out the granite collection. But I'd also like to use other materials. I remember Ken Dryden talking about Rejean Houle coming from the mining areas of Rouyn Noranda. I'd like to do a stick as a tribute to Houle, using metals like copper and zinc from that area." And that's just the beginning.

"I'm always finding stick blades washed up on the beaches around here, they're polished like sea glass. My ultimate stick would be a shaft in a type of bluish glass with a variety of these curves in it. Then I'd set up a situation where the light would go through the sticks, totally natural and unaffected."

It's time for Davey's visitor to return to the ferry and the urban hubbub across the harbour. The sculptor offers a parting gift: a puck made from Labrador Black granite. On one side, Davey has carved the sniper's eye of Maurice Richard; the Rocket's ocular orbit flashes demonically out of the pitch. On the other side of the puck he has sculpted Gordie Howe's notorious elbow, menace jutting from the granite.

"Some people say to me, 'Mike, you'll kill the art by being so specific.' But I like the specific nature of this. I want to cast a stick as a piece of ice made out of beer. Or the blade made out of Canadian Club, and the shaft made out of beer. Wouldn't that be interesting?"

Considering the spell hockey casts over the nation, Hockey Witch, a cheeky 1995 exhibit at Toronto's Linda Genereux Gallery, shouldn't have come as too great a surprise. Crossed goalie sticks with brooms of twigs where the blade should be . . . the stick's logo changed from Sher-Wood to Her-Wood . . . a cauldron of boiling pucks . . . a pointy witches' hat with a brim encrusted with tiny hockey sticks made of maple keys and twigs . . . a hockey witch with a single chrysalis eye, fish for hair, a frog on a flaming cauldron . . .

Hockey has been described as the pagan religion of Canada, and that makes perfect sense to the creative team of Fastwurms (also known as Kim Kozzi and Dai Skuse) that produced Hockey Witch and other dark tributes to the game. The two artists can think of nothing more divine than grabbing their sticks and some unconventional apparel to play in a league called Fi-O-Fire, a collection of Toronto artists mad about hockey.

"Our explanation for Hockey Witch was that it was our two favourite religions," admits Skuse, forty-six, whose farm lies in the rolling countryside near Guelph. "Hockey approaches a religion in Canada. The passions brought into play are out of line with the activity itself. And the pagan religion is ours in terms of witchcraft, because we're both kind of witches, which is an oddity in the art scene." And in the hockey scene, one might add.

Skuse and Kozzi have been practitioners of the Old Religion for some time; their eleven-acre farm even has a swamp. "Witches like swamps," admits Skuse, "and there's more bats out here." Their Turtle Pond floor mosaic in the new wing of the Metro Toronto Convention Centre – replete with frogs, turtles, and lily pads – shows the influence that witchcraft has had on their work. But only in the last few years – when they were criticized for borrowing First Nations culture – have they spoken publicly about their belief in this European tradition, which predates Christianity in most countries.

The decision to "out" themselves as ardent fans of hockey's rude culture was also late in coming. Would the simple beauty of the ash stick be frowned upon by an avant-garde community? They needn't have worried; they soon

Like so many Canadian kids, Dai Skuse (left) grew up playing
and loving the game. Unlike most, he became an artist
fascinated by hockey imagery

found like minds among their fellow artists. Now when they
play hockey, they wear sweaters decorated with bats and cats
and crescent moons.

Kozzi sees parallels between hockey and witchcraft.
"They're both hard-to-read social phenomena. Obviously
we're putting something that's rather obscure, witchcraft, up
against something that's like a mass religion. But it's an unac-
knowledged pagan religion, and often people try to be quiet
about it. One of the things we discuss when we're having a
beer after a game is how hockey itself has maintained a pretty

straight demeanour. I haven't heard of any gay players writing tell-all memoirs and getting attention for it. It's still a very strange world that way – know what I mean?"

"What we found in our hockey league," adds Skuse, "is that there are lots of people in art who were afraid to admit they liked hockey because it's associated with goonery and the kind of sentiment that gets expressed in editorials by Don Cherry. I brought up how Cherry has this kind of anti-sissy thing going, yet he dresses like an Edwardian dandy – the high point of crossover between gay culture and sport."

While Kozzi never played hockey as a young woman in Ottawa, Skuse grew up in the same city loving the sport. Unfortunately, when his Welsh-born father went out to buy him skates, he came home with second-hand figure skates. "It was a 'Boy Named Sue' situation," he laughs, "where I ended up playing goal in public school. That's the only thing the skates were good for. My dad either didn't want or couldn't afford to buy good goalie equipment. Then, around Grade Seven, Bobby Hull came out with the banana curve, so every damn kid in class was steaming his stick and bending it under door frames. Next thing you know, you're on the ice wearing this cruddy equipment like Gump Worsley – a little piece of leather on your chest and all that – and some guy would unload with the banana stick. That's when I called it quits. I had a high pain tolerance, but that was too much. You walk around with these big green-blue welts on your chest. It wasn't cool."

Years later, when friends told him they were playing in Toronto's High Park, Skuse – by then a budding artist – decided to give hockey another try. Together with Carlo

Cesta, Lisa Neighbor, and Brent Roe, they braved the outdoor ice of Grenadier Pond in what Jennifer McMackern described as "a tableau for a Breugel painting with everybody and his dog out on the ice." To Skuse's surprise, there were some fine players in Toronto's exploding art-hockey scene, including a former Junior A player who'd spent time in the hitherto unknown Basque League in Spain. Those games on Grenadier Pond eventually turned into a weekly game at McCormick Arena where, among their peers, some of the city's finest artists, male and female, made like Wayne Gretzky.

"I find that people who don't play often get more carried away and dangerous," laughs Skuse. "They'll be skating on one foot going into the boards at full speed with their stick over their heads – having just missed the puck and swooping back to get it." Being artists, of course, they also can't help making aesthetic judgements. A cheap goal is likely to spark the cry, "There's no irony in that!"

"People dress up," says Skuse. "A lot of people wear drag when they're playing. And there are a lot of references to obscure hockey stuff. My one buddy would be wearing, like, early Russian. Someone else would be wearing shirts from obscure teams in the west. I used to have a pair of gloves that had 'Love/Hate' painted on them."

The weekly games eventually inspired the players to take their passion beyond the rink. Paul Petro, owner of the Paul Petro Contemporary Art Gallery on Yonge Street in Toronto, was looking to create a display of hockey art, with proceeds going to help minor hockey. Petro's dad had played for Canada with the East York Lyndhursts at the

World Championships in 1954 – the first year the Soviet Union competed – and he liked the idea of letting loose these creative people on the national game. "Scott Young used to come over to my house to ask my dad about the Lyndhurst Motors," Petro said at the time. "The whole hockey mythology is part of my background."

Petro and Jennifer McMackern decided that to help raise money for underprivileged tyke players at Moss Park, everyone in the free-floating Fi-O-Fire shinny game would interpret the hockey stick in his or her own way, the results to be sold at a charity auction. The show would be called Sac de Hockey, with each exhibit accompanied by a photo of the artist posing with the Stanley Cup at the Hockey Hall of Fame.

The results of this stick deconstruction were as individual as the artists. There was one stick festooned with tiny Christmas lights encrusted in wax, another covered with foam. One stick was carved into quarters with the pieces loosely held together by wire; yet another had a flashlight affixed to the top of the blade for "night skating." There were sticks with extension cables and sticks covered in cow skin, and a camp fire fuelled by Bauer sticks.

"Some of the sticks were extremely quirky," recalls Skuse. "I remember one that was folded up and turned almost into a basket – the blade was cut into many fine pieces of wood and they were all folded around like a nest. It's what you can get when artists are trying to impress each other. It's a very odd sculptural concept that you wouldn't expect."

But the pièce de résistance was probably Skuse's own tribute to legendary tough guy Dave "Tiger" Williams, who played for Toronto and Vancouver in the 1970s and '80s. "At that time I really had a thing about Tiger Williams. I had the stick upholstered in tiger fabric, and I attached one of his rookie cards on the tag. I also put a strap on it so you could carry it over your shoulder. Artists are interested in cultural phenomena. Tiger Williams is a throwback to that '70s period of hockey when they wore the ridiculous moustaches and all. And the way he was so outspoken – I admired that."

The critics loved the collection of unlikely sticks. "It's an amazing display," said *NOW*, a Toronto magazine that specializes in covering Toronto's offbeat cultural scene. "It's an eclectic but electrifying show, clearly born out of a deep-rooted love of hockey among all those involved. It's a perfect show for the Canadian winter."

The American writer Ralph Earley has said that history will remember the United States for three things: the Constitution, baseball, and jazz. What lasting gifts has Canada bestowed on the world? Hockey for one. The canoe for another. Had Joseph Conrad sent Marlow up a Canadian river to discover Colonel Kurtz and the heart of darkness, no doubt he'd have placed his brooding protagonist in a birch-bark canoe. Nothing speaks to the soul of this nation like the canoe – handed down by First Nations people, quickly adopted by the newly arrived Europeans. Nothing, that is, but the hockey stick, first carved by the same indigenous people.

"The canoe was one of the few gifts the natives were able to give the white men that they didn't already have," Geoff Currie, an Ontario artist, says. Currie has brought these two

Canadian symbols together in a remote corner of Georgian Bay. Painstakingly assembled from hockey sticks over twenty-five years, the Fedorov Canoe (as Currie christened it), made of hockey sticks, spends its winters upturned on the shore, under a snow-covered lean-to, in the stillness of the wilderness near Go Home Bay, gathering strength for another summer. Currie collected more than 400 ash-handled hockey sticks to fashion his unique vessel. "I used to be known as 'the idiot who's collecting sticks.' I had people saving them for me all over the place. One day I had all these hockey sticks and put them in the water taxi to get to my place at Go Home Bay. The locals couldn't quite believe I was making something out of them.

"I am not a commercial person, I'm an artist first. Once, I started making these monumental rock installations out of stones I found on the beach in Toronto. I found these paving stones washed up on the beach and made an amphitheatre park with them. It must have had thousands of cobblestones. Judging from the stone, some of them could have been 500 years old, ones brought over as ballast from Scotland in the early days of the city. They used them to pave the early streets and then dumped them in the harbour. One of those cobblestones is probably worth ten or fifteen dollars now. When I was finished, the thing was about eighty feet in diameter. People landing at the Island Airport said they could see it from the planes. I didn't get paid for it. I just ended up doing free art for the city."

The Fedorov canoe did not spring from a boyhood of crisp Saskatchewan winters listening to "Hockey Night in Canada" on the crystal set. Currie was born in Seattle in

1956 and moved around the United States with his family to wherever his parents were working. The one constant was summers in far-off Georgian Bay. "My father was a teacher, so we had the entire summer off. My mother was the local postmistress in the summers. But I never played hockey till I was ten. I embraced the game once we moved to Canada so I could keep up with my friends. I found the skating sensation quite something. Now I play a lot of hockey. When I hurt the MCL [medial collateral ligament] in my knee one winter and couldn't play, I used to wake up at night dreaming I was playing hockey."

Before embarking on the canoe project, Currie read countless books and studied the traditional art of canoe-making with experts, getting all the help he could find to fashion his 18-foot, 4-inch racing canoe. He had time on his hands in Group of Seven country as he tried to make a living as a landscape artist; during long winter nights, in an isolated corner of Ontario not served by roads, he steamed the sticks he'd collected – much as the original stick manufacturers had done – stripping each one lengthwise to get two pieces for the ribs of the canoe. "I was amazed at what you could do with wood that was steam bent. I mean, you can hold up a steamed stick at the ends and it will sag like pasta in the middle. You can tie it in a knot if the wood is thin enough. That's what I liked about the ash – the wood has a nice straight grain, and it's very good for bending."

Currie used common Cooper or CCM sticks for the ribs. For the gunwales he chose red Titan Wayne Gretzky sticks that flash their gaudiness inside the canoe. A Mike Bossy autograph from one of his Titans adorns the keel. With the

Methinks this Quebec City demonstrator doth protest in a particularly Canadian way, using a hockey stick to fire a canister back at the police

skeleton in place, Currie had to master birch bark. Harvesting the white-grey bark proved difficult. "My brain was always running ahead of my ability to get materials. You need the innermost layer. The best kind of bark, the kind natives used, was winter bark – you could etch it once it was in place. They used to do all sorts of fancy designs in their canoes. I wanted a more rounded bottom than in the traditional canoe. Because the boat is twenty-three inches at the beam, as opposed to the traditional twenty inches, I needed forty-five-inch strips to wrap around the gunwales. But you have to look hard to find enough of it in long strips." Slowly, carefully, Currie harvested the bark and painstakingly applied it to the ribs. The great names of stick makers provide a rowdy chorus of colour against the white bark of the hull. "The water skiers around here, their boats all have these fancy paint jobs. So I put sparkle paint along one side of my boat.

"The natives used to sink their canoes in the fall with stones," Currie adds. "In spring, when the ice melted, they'd bring the canoes up. That way the bark wouldn't dry out." He considered submerging his own beloved canoe beneath the icy waters of Georgian Bay, then thought better of it. "I was afraid some of the Titan and Cooper sticks I used couldn't take being underwater all winter. They might have warped." He sighs. "But I don't think it's good for the birch bark to dry out, either.

"When I get a hole in the bark, I use epoxy glue, not the ancient techniques of the natives. They used to carry bear grease mixed with black spruce pitch for patching their canoes. They could apply it at night and by morning the grease would be dry and the hole repaired. They'd also use floorboards in the canoe; when they came to a rocky passage or a rapids in the river, they'd attach the floorboards to the outside of the canoe to protect the birch bark from being ripped. I haven't put floor boards in my canoe. I have to be careful when I get close to shore that the rocks don't rip the bark."

With proper care and storage, some of the best birch-bark canoes have lasted a hundred years and more. While Currie would love for his canoe to last that long, he shakes his head when asked if the hockey sticks will outlive the bark. "I'd say the canoe will last a minimum of fifteen years. It all depends on the ash in the sticks. I'd like someone to give it a home when I'm not using it any more."

The canoe is "built for speed," he says, "just like Sergei Fedorov. That year he won the Hart Trophy as most valuable player [1994], he was outstanding. He became my favourite player. I have his number 91 sweater. He's a player who uses his speed and skill. I just started calling it the Fedorov Canoe and it seemed to stick." He pauses. "Since the Anna Kournikova thing, he's now only *one* of my favourite players. I didn't like him going out with a fourteen-year-old very much."

Currie's unorthodox design means the canoe is taller and narrower than most, making it tippy in rough conditions. How would it race? The Fedorov Canoe quickly proved its worth in local regattas. "I had two firsts and a tie for first in the regattas I entered," Currie says proudly. Winning helped counter the reputation Currie had acquired as an eccentric. "I guess I'm known as a wacky guy locally. No one could quite believe what I was doing. But when they saw the canoe completed with all the hockey emblems, people were quite taken with it."

Currie spends his winters in the city now, but come spring he'll again head north to Georgian Bay, near Parry Sound, the town that spawned Bobby Orr. Once the snow has melted from the lean-to, he'll uncover his prized creation, patch the cracked and desiccated birch bark, and slip the bow back into the water. He'll shove off and begin paddling, rhythmic as Paul Coffey skating. He'll stick close to shore in the many inlets, just as the Huron did hundreds of years ago. The bow will slice the waves as crisply as a skate blade on a frozen pond.

Out on the bay, the modern speedboats with their fibreglass hulls and aluminum railings will bounce over the water with hardly a sideways glance at the man making his way, stroke by stroke, in the hockey-stick canoe with its bright colours dancing in the sun. But Currie will be alert to the churning waves they throw up and turn his bow into the wake so that his canoe won't be swamped.

BIBLIOGRAPHY

Brodeur, Denis. *Goalies: Guardians of the Net.* Toronto: Key Porter, 1995.

Diamond, Dan (ed.). *Total Hockey.* Toronto: Total Sports Publications, 2000.

Dryden, Ken. *The Game.* Toronto: McClelland & Stewart, 1982.

Duhatschek, Eric, et al. *Hockey Chronicles.* Toronto: Key Porter, 2000.

Farrar, John Laird. *Trees in Canada.* Toronto: Fitzhenry & Whiteside, 1995.

Fischler, Stan and Shirley (eds.). *Great Book of Hockey.* Lincolnwood, Illinois: Publications International, 1991.

Granatstein, J.L. *Who Killed Canadian History?* Toronto: HarperCollins, 1998.

Gwyn, Richard. *Nationalism Without Walls.* Toronto: McClelland & Stewart, 1995.

Heinrich, Bernd. *The Trees in My Forest*. New York: HarperCollins, 1997.

Howe, Gordie and Colleen. *And Howe. . . .* Traverse City, Michigan: Power Play Productions, 1995.

Hunter, Douglas. *A Breed Apart*. Toronto: Viking, 1995.

Hunter, Douglas. *Champions*. Toronto: Penguin Studio, 1997.

Irvin, Dick. *In the Crease*. Toronto: McClelland & Stewart, 1995.

Jenkins, Phil. *An Acre of Time*. Toronto: Macfarlane Walter & Ross, 1996.

Liebman, Glenn. *Hockey Shorts*. New York: Contemporary Books, 1996.

MacGregor, Roy. *The Home Team*. Toronto: Viking Press, 1995.

MacKay, Donald. *The Lumberjacks*. Toronto: Natural Heritage, 1998.

McKinley, Michael. *Hockey Hall of Fame Legends*. Toronto: Viking, 1993.

McPhee, John. *Annals of the Former World*. New York: Farrar, Straus and Giroux, 1999.

MacSkimming, Roy. *Cold War: The Amazing Canada-Soviet Hockey Series of 1972*. Vancouver: Greystone, 1996.

Morton, Desmond. *A Short History of Canada*. Toronto: McClelland & Stewart, 1997.

Peattie, Donald Culross. *A Natural History of Trees*. Boston: Houghton Mifflin, 1964.

Pelchat, Gilles. *Sher-Wood et son batisseur Leopold Drolet*. Sherwood, Quebec: GGC Editions, 2000.

Percival, Lloyd. *The Hockey Handbook*. McClelland & Stewart, 1992.

Raffan, James. *Bark, Skin and Cedar*. Toronto: HarperCollins, 1999.

Roxborough, Henry. *The Stanley Cup Story*. Toronto: Ryerson, 1965.

Shostak, Peter. *Hockey . . . Under Winter Skies*. Victoria: Yalenka Enterprises, 2000.

Traill, Catherine Parr. *Pearls and Pebbles*. Toronto: Natural Heritage, 1999.

Vaughan, Garth. *The Puck Starts Here*. Fredericton: Goose Lane, 1996.

INDEX

The text of this book was set in Sabon, Jan Tschichold's interpretation of Garamond, originally released in metal by Stempel in 1964 and later digitized by Adobe. Renaissance letter forms and large x-height make Sabon ideal for book setting.

Book design by Terri Fong